The Gene Book

Explorations in the Code of Life

Bassim Hamadeh, CEO and Publisher
John Remington, Senior Field Acquisitions Editor
Michelle Piehl, Project Editor
Abbey Hastings, Associate Production Editor
Concept Development, Senior Graphic Designer
Stephanie Kohl, Licensing Associate
Gustavo Youngberg, Interior Designer
Natalie Piccotti, Senior Marketing Manager
Kassie Graves, Vice President of Editorial
Jamie Giganti, Director of Academic Publishing

Printed in the United States of America.

ISBN: 978-1-5165-2101-2 (pbk) / 978-1-5165-2102-9 (br) / 978-1-5165-4524-7 (al)

The Gene Book

Explorations in the Code of Life

By Sarah Adelaide Crawford

cognella® | ACADEMIC PUBLISHING

This book is dedicated to my dear father, Thomas A. Crawford, who loved both science and books—this one is for you.

CONTENTS

Chapter 1

Genetics Discoveries: Meeting Mendel
What Mendel's Discoveries Taught Us About Inheritance

Figure 1.1

Garden pea botanical print

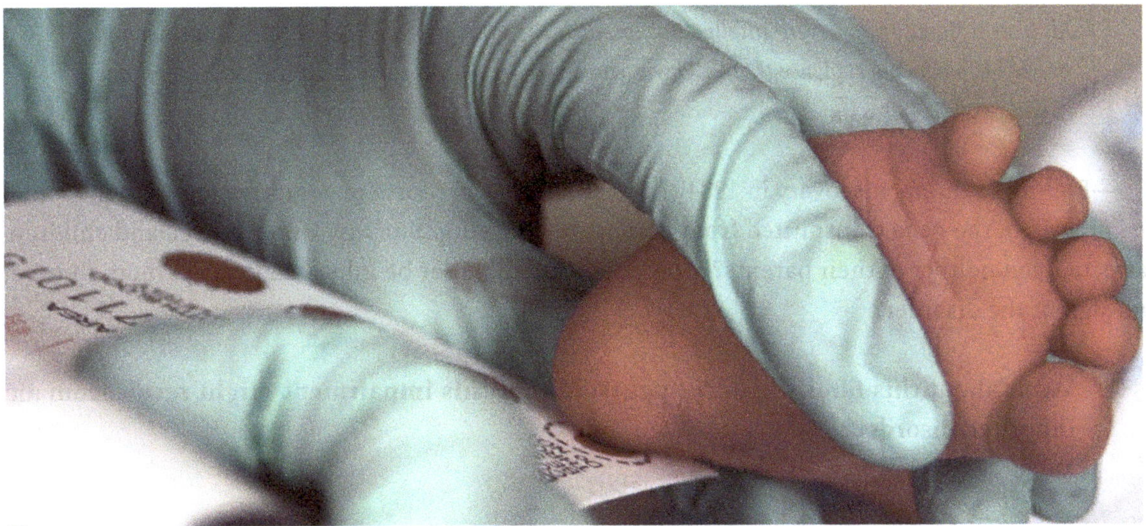

Figure 1.2

Newborn is tested for PKU

The Discovery of Phenylketonuria (1934)

Borgny and Harry Egeland lived in Oslo and were married in 1923. They eventually begot two children both of who developed mental retardation. By 1934, the oldest, a girl by the name of Liv, was 6½ years old. She is described as being ... very restless, always fluttering about from one thing to another without issue. She is able to say some words which are understood by her family but she does not talk in sentences. (See Figure 1.2.)

The youngest was a 4-year-old boy by the name of Dag. His level of impairment was even worse than his sister. He is barely able to sit upright when supported. His head is inclined to drop to one side. He is unable to talk, expels some inarticulate sounds, cries and smiles, wants to play and to be entertained. He is unable to eat without assistance or to chew solid food and must accordingly be nourished on a liquid diet. Interestingly, their parents also noticed an atypical odor associated with both children.

Subsequently, the Egelands contacted a doctor they'd heard about named Asborn Følling. Having postulated that the children's mental retardation was somehow related to the presence of the phenylpyruvic acid in their urine, Følling set out to explore whether this relationship was present in other impaired children as well. Følling found eight more individuals, including two additional sibling groups.

In addition to the urine similarity, he noted that the individuals also shared other characteristics. They tended to have fair complexions, eczema, broad shoulders, stooping figure, and spastic gait.

All also suffered from severe intellectual impairment. The genealogical data from this sample provided convincing evidence that PKU was passed by simple autosomal recessive gene inheritance. (Centerwall, 2000)

So—Følling's seminal discovery in 1934 showed that a severe form of cognitive impairment could be inherited, the gene transmitted from parents to offspring. But why were the Egeland children affected, but neither of their parents? How could this disorder be inherited if the parents showed no sign of the disorder?

1. **What about this family history suggested that this impairment might result from an inherited disorder?**

A Visit to Mendel's Garden

Gregor Johann Mendel (1822–1884). (Courtesy of Professor William Bateson, London.)

Figure 1.3

Gregor Mendel

To answer this important question, we have to move farther back in time, to a monastery in Brno, now the Czech Republic, and visit a 19th-century monk busy at work in the garden (see Figure 1.3). He is studying the garden pea (see Figure 1.1), and how its traits are transmitted from one plant generation to the next. He could not have known at the time that his discoveries would explain far more than inheritance in the garden pea, but rather would become a blueprint for life, explaining how genes are passed from parents to offspring for almost all forms of life.

So let's visit with Gregor Mendel for a while and see what his work is telling us about inheritance. Let's start with the color of the flowers. Garden peas come in two colors: white and purple. Mendel makes an interesting observation.

When he crosses pure purple plants with pure white plants, ALL the offspring are purple. Mendel has concluded that "purple flower color" is dominant to "white flower color" in the garden pea (see Figure 1.4). He repeats this experiment for several additional traits in the garden pea and reaches the same conclusion every time: One form of the trait is always **dominant** to the other. He calls the "hidden" trait **recessive.** This observation becomes Mendel's **Law of Dominance.**

2. **Show the genetic cross for plant height. The parents are pure tall X pure short. Use symbols to show the genetic cross.**
3. **Why are all the offspring tall, even though one of the parents is short?**

Mendel wasn't finished yet. He decides to take things a step further. He takes the tall plants produced by crossing the pure tall and pure short parents and crosses these offspring to see what happens. He probably expected that this new generation would all be tall because both parents were tall. But—and what a surprise—some plants in this second generation are short! How could this happen?

4. **When the offspring from question 1-1 are crossed what are the genotypes and phenotypes of the offspring produced by this cross?**
5. **Why do we see short plants produced by tall parents if short is recessive to tall?**

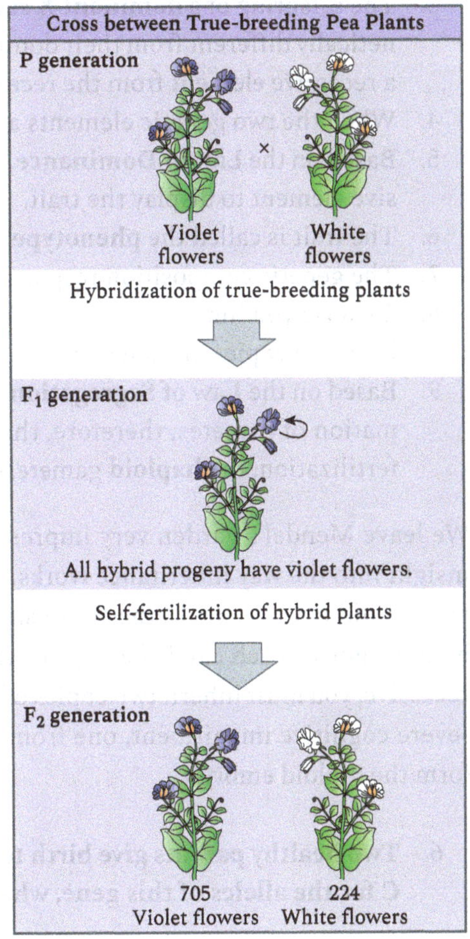

Figure 1.4

Single gene cross

Mendel needs to figure this out. So he decides to count the number of tall and short plants and he finds that about 3/4 of the plants are tall and 1/4 are short. So he repeats this experiment, studying this and other traits in the garden pea, and always sees the same thing: About 3/4 display the dominant trait and 1/4 are recessive (see Figure 1.4).

Based on this evidence, Mendel devises a theory: The reappearance of the recessive trait shows that the genetic element specifying shortness was present in the tall parents; there must be TWO elements—one from each parent—that determines the inheritance of a trait! The fact that a new combination of these genetic elements could produce a short plant suggested that genetic factors can separate during the formation of gametes and produce novel combinations in the offspring. He calls this the **Law of Segregation.**

So Let's Summarize What Mendel Has Told Us So Far

1. If you cross a **pure dominant** with a **recessive trait**, all offspring will show the dominant trait. However, the offspring will still carry a copy of the recessive element.
2. In the language of genetics, a pure dominant is **homozygous**, having two copies of the dominant element.

3. The offspring of a **dominant X recessive** cross will show the dominant trait, but will be genetically different from their dominant parent, because they are not pure but have inherited a recessive element from the recessive parent.
4. When the two genetic elements are different, this is called **heterozygous.**
5. Based on the **Law of Dominance**, recessive individuals must have TWO copies of the recessive element to display the trait.
6. The trait is called the **phenotype.**
7. The genetic composition responsible for the trait is called the **genotype.**
8. Because you inherit one genetic element from your mother and one from your father, you have two copies of each genetic element. Therefore, you are **diploid.**
9. Based on the **Law of Segregation**, the two paired genetic elements separate during the formation of gametes; therefore, the gametes have only one copy and are called **haploid**. At fertilization, the **haploid** gametes—sperm and egg—fuse to form a **diploid** embryo.

We leave Mendel's garden very impressed. Such simple experiments have provided such great insight into the way inheritance works. Now Følling's discovery makes more sense. The Egeland parents did not have PKU, they both showed the **dominant** normal brain function, but each was heterozygous—each carried a copy of the defective **recessive** genetic element. Because PKU is **recessive**, you must inherit two copies of the defective element to show the abnormal phenotype—severe cognitive impairment, one from each parent, in the **haploid** sperm and egg fertilized to form the diploid embryo.

6. **Two healthy parents give birth to a child diagnosed with cystic fibrosis. Using the letter C for the alleles of this gene, what are the parents' genotypes?**

    - **Cc and Cc**
    - **Cc and CC**
    - **cc and cc**
    - **CC and cc**

We are anxious to return to Mendel's garden, to learn more about inheritance, but first we need some tools. The first is the Punnett Square, which shows us how we can combine gametes in genetic crosses and observe the expected results. Let's learn how to prepare and analyze a Punnett Square (see Figure 1.5).

Using the **Punnett Square**, we see where Mendel's 3:1 ratio comes from. It results from a **monohybrid cross** where both parents are heterozygous. Regardless of whether we are studying the inheritance of height in the pea plant or PKU in humans, the pattern is exactly the same.

Why is one form of a trait **dominant** and the other is **recessive**? What causes this?

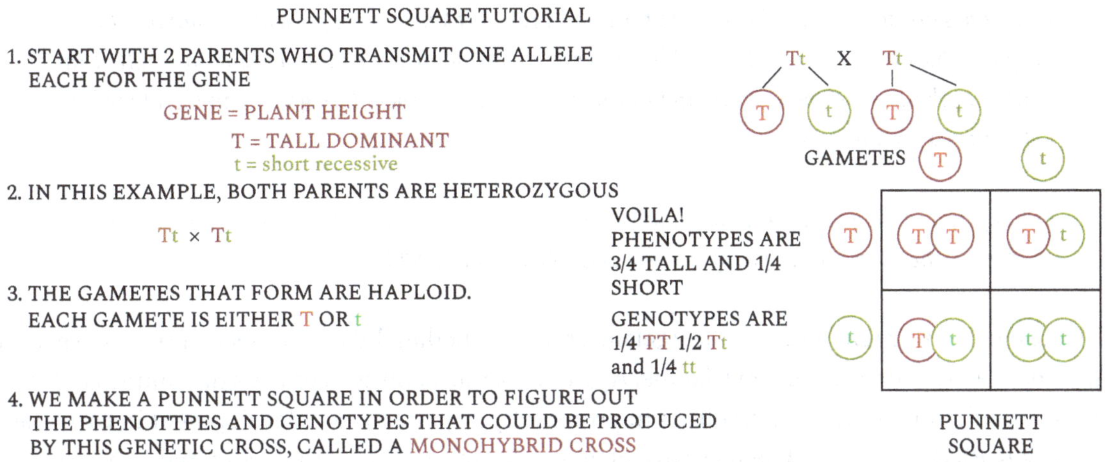

Figure 1.5

Tutorial: Punnett Square

Mendel had no idea. But Følling's research on PKU led to an explanation of why this genetic disorder is **recessive**. Let's visit his laboratory where he is conducting biochemical studies on the Egeland children's urine samples (see Figure 1.6).

Figure 1.6

Følling's biochemistry lab

While routinely testing the children's urine for ketones, however, Følling made a strange, unexpected discovery. To test for ketones, a solution of aqueous ferric chloride is added to the urine. Typically, no ketones are present and the mixture turns red-brown. If ketones are present, the mixture turns purple or burgundy. Mixing ferric chloride with the urine of the Egeland children resulted in neither of these reactions. Instead, their urine immediately turned dark green and then faded in color after a few minutes.

Følling worked diligently for a month to isolate the substance. Another six weeks were necessary to identify the substance as phenylpyruvic acid. (Centerwall, 2000)

Well, the biochemistry showed that the Egeland children's bodies did not produce the enzyme needed to metabolize the amino acid phenylalanine. Apparently, the inability to process this amino acid leads to its accumulation in the body resulting in profoundly impaired brain development in early life.

So why is PKU recessive? The recessive element is a mutant gene that can't make the enzyme. The Egeland parents were **heterozygous** carriers; they each had one normal and one nonfunctional copy of this gene. The children inherited a copy of the nonfunctional element from each parent—no enzyme—leading to PKU.

Wait a minute—you may ask. If that's the case, then because the Egeland parents were carriers, and had only one functional copy of the gene, their bodies should produce only half as much enzyme as noncarriers who have two functional copies of the gene. Good question! As a matter of fact, Følling is studying just this question in his laboratory right now.

So—the Egeland parents only produce 1/2 the normal amount of enzyme—but it's enough to do the job—so the Egeland parents are normal—**heterozygous dominant**—whereas their two children have two copies of the nonfunctional gene and have the **recessive phenotype**, PKU (see Figure 1.7).

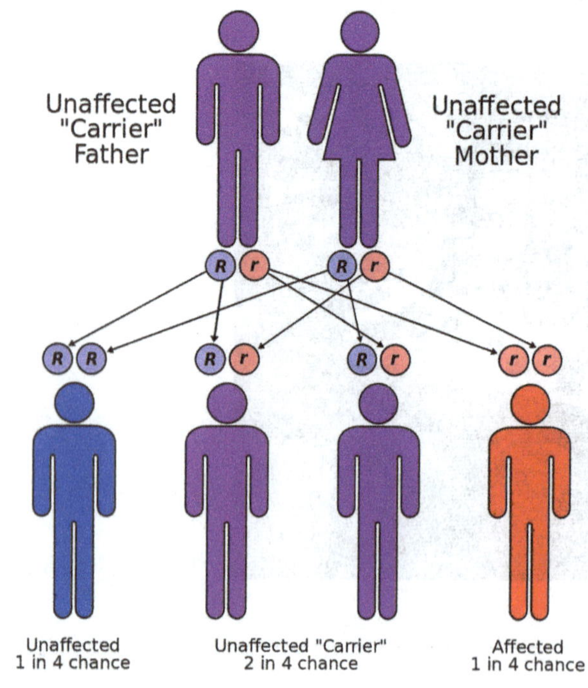

Figure 1.7

Single gene inheritance in humans

7. **If a disorder is dominant, and one parent is affected, what are the parental genotypes if they produce one child who is affected with this disorder and one who is not?**

   a. **DD and dd**
   b. **Dd and dd**
   c. **Dd and Dd**
   d. **DD and Dd**

More than Mendel

We are so excited to learn so much about inheritance. Mendel was truly amazing! Are all genes inherited this way—dominant or recessive? Actually, no; inheritance can be a little more complex than that. For example, some traits show **incomplete dominance**. Mendel noticed that the inheritance pattern for some traits resembled neither parent, but was somewhere in between. In 1900, another botanist, Karl Correns, described this phenomenon in four o'clock plants. If he took a red flower plant and crossed it with a white flower plant, all the progeny plants had pink flowers! Let's see how this works (see Figure 1.8).

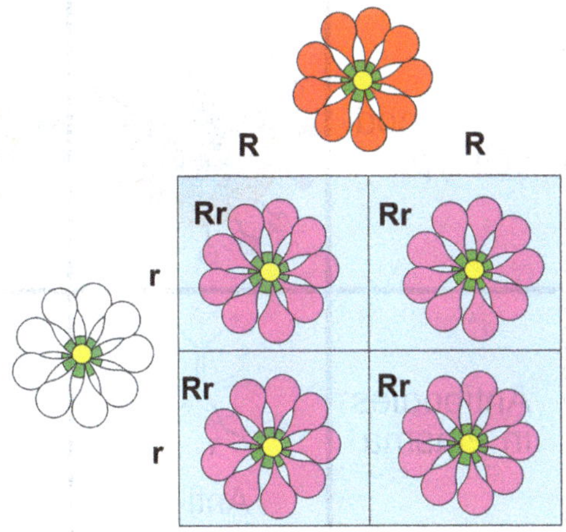

Figure 1.8

Incomplete dominance

8. **Four o'clock plants come in three colors: red, white, and pink. What is the expected phenotypic ratio for the progeny of two pink flower plants in which flower color is incompletely dominant?**

- **A 3:1**
- **B 1:1:1**
- **C 1:2:1**

There's another interesting form of inheritance: It's called **co-dominance**. Human blood types are inherited this way (see Figure 1.9). We're going to visit Landsteiner's laboratory to learn all about it. More than a century ago, Landsteiner defined four blood types in humans: A, B, AB, and O. He discovers that blood type is inherited and it shows some unusual patterns. He is studying a patient who has Type AB blood. To his surprise, he finds that his patient's mother is Type A and his father is Type B. Their child expresses BOTH these traits—he is blood type AB. This type of inheritance is called **co-dominance**. Landsteiner realizes that the boy inherited the A form of the gene from his mother and the B form of the gene from his father. But neither version of the gene dominates the phenotype. Both forms of the gene equally contribute to the phenotype.

Research on more patients' blood types shows that a different story occurs in regard to the inheritance of Type O blood. Landsteiner is seeing a patient today who has type O blood. He examines the little girl's parent case histories and finds that her mother has type A blood and her father has type B blood. The doctor is perplexed: Where did the type O phenotype come from? Landsteiner goes back to the laboratory and reviews the patient history more carefully. It turns out that both the little girls' grandmothers had type O blood. The story was beginning to make sense. Both the

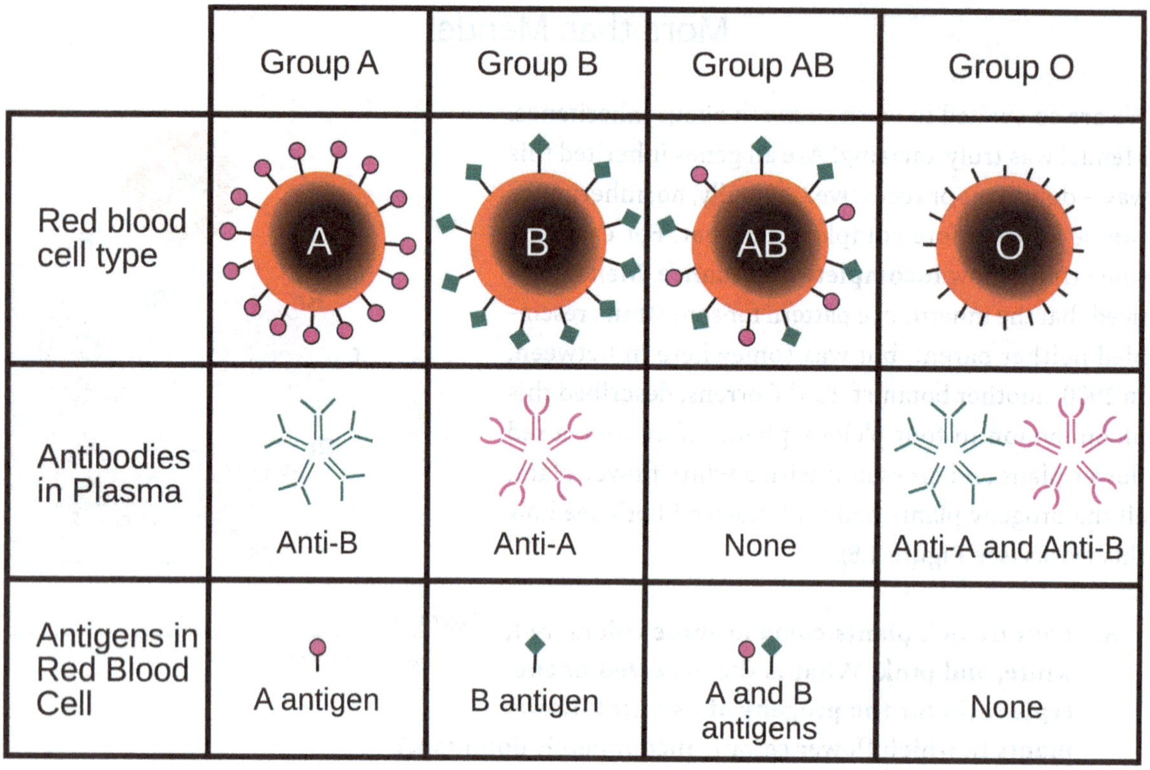

Figure 1.9

Human blood types

girl's parents are carriers of the O form of the gene, hence they are heterozygous. However, neither has type O blood because O is recessive to both A and B, resulting in the observation that the girl's mother is type A and her father is type B. O is recessive to both these forms of the gene!

9. **Two parents with type A blood can produce offspring with which blood types?**

  a. **Type A only**
  b. **Type A and Type O**
  c. **Type O only**

This makes a lot of sense, but we ask Dr. Landsteiner one more question before we go. We learned from Mendel that each person has two copies of every gene, but Dr. Landsteiner's research shows that there are THREE gene copies for blood type. How can this be? Dr. Landsteiner smiles; he has heard this question many times before. He explains to us that, although each individual has only two copies of every gene, there may be more than two possible gene types in the population as a whole. This is called **multiple alleles**. An **allele** is another name for gene copy. In the human species, there are three copies of the allele for blood type. Each of us has two; which ones we inherit depend on the blood types of our parents. Now the entire story makes sense.

Dr. Landsteiner has even more exciting news for us! He has discovered a gene called the Rh factor. An individual can be Rh+ or Rh-. The inheritance pattern for the Rh factor is another example of Mendel's **Law of Dominance**. Rh+ is dominant over Rh-. His next patient is a young boy who is Rh-. The boy's parents want to know how their son inherited this **phenotype**. The doctor examines the parents' medical histories: The mother is blood type A, Rh+ and the father is Type B, Rh-. He explains to the family that the boy, who is Type A, Rh- inherited one **recessive** allele from his father and one from his mother, who must be **heterozygous** Rh+. This makes a lot of sense, a case of simple dominance. Just as they are about to leave the doctor's office, the boy's father notices something unusual. Because his son is Rh- like him, why does he have a different blood type, A instead of B? Is he really this man's son? Now Dr. Landsteiner starts to laugh! Didn't Professor Mendel explain that to you? He suggested we all pay the Father of Genetics another visit.

We find Prof. Mendel busy working in his garden as usual. But he takes the time to explain what's going on. The boy's father is his biological parent, Mendel asserts immediately, putting us all at ease. He takes us to the greenhouse and shows us his records of plant matings (see Figure 1.10). Starting with a parental generation called P1 he explored the inheritance of two different traits in the same plant family: height and flower color. He crossed a pure tall, purple flower plant with a short white flower plant and observed that the of the P1 generation, called the F1 generation, were all tall with purple flowers. No surprises there, based on the **Law of Dominance**. We certainly hope the story is going to get more interesting than this! Mendel then goes on to say that he crossed the **F1 dihybrids** (both parents are heterozygous for each of the two genes) and observed that the next generation called the F2 was composed mostly of tall plants with purple flowers. A few showed the double recessive phenotype, short with white flowers.

But then he observed the most amazing thing! Some of the plants showed combinations of traits that were not observed in their

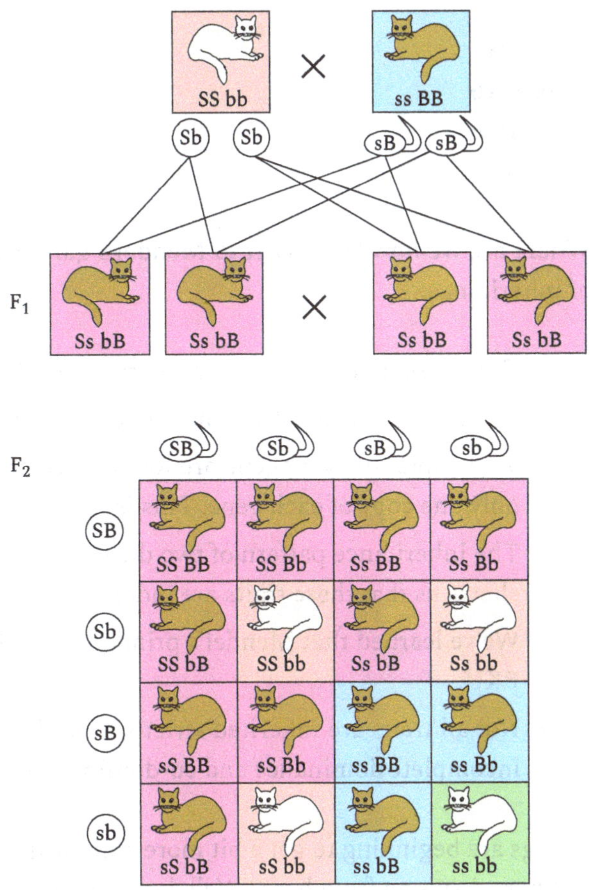

Figure 1.10

Dihybrid cross

parents—the F1—or their grandparents—the P1 generation. He shows us a plant from this F2 generation that is tall but has white flowers. And then another that was short with purple flowers. How could a tall plant in this plant family have white flowers when only the short grandparents had white flowers? How could some of the tall plants have purple flowers? The tall ancestors had only purple flowers. Mendel says he suddenly realized that these traits—plant height and flower color—were inherited as separate genetic elements so that all combinations of the two could be produced. He called this the **Law of Independent Assortment.**

So now we know what happened when the little boy was shown to be Rh- with Type A blood whereas his father was Rh- with Type B blood and his mother was Rh+ and Type A blood. In humans, the genes for blood type and Rh factor are inherited as separate genetic elements. We see how the **Law of Independent Assortment** explains a lot about how traits are inherited.

10. **If both parents are IAi and Rh+/-, what fraction of their offspring can be expected to have Type A blood and Rh- phenotypes?**

    a. **1/4**
    b. **9/16**
    c. **1/16**
    d. **3/16**

Where are we now? Our visit to Mendel's garden has taught us some really important concepts of inheritance:

- Genes are inherited as discrete units—each gene defines a trait.
- Genes may consist of alternative forms: dominant or recessive.
- Two copies of every gene are found in the cell—except when gametes form—they contain only one copy of each gene. This is the **Law of Segregation.**
- The inheritance pattern of two different genes (flower color and plant height, for example) shows us that these traits are independently inherited.
- We've learned that Mendel's principles can be applied to human inheritance, for example, PKU.
- Not all traits are inherited strictly according to the **Law of Dominance**. We learned about incomplete dominance and co-dominance.

Things are beginning to get a bit more complex!

Where do we go from here? Well, let's see. It looks like we're going to be exploring family trees and playing genetic dice! We hurry off to Chapter 2.

References

Centerwall, S. and Centerwall, W. "The Discovery of Phenylketonuria," *Pediatrics* 105 no.1 (2000): 89–103.

Christ, Shawn E., "Asbjørn Følling and the Discovery of Phenylketonuria," *Journal of the History of the Neurosciences* 12, no. 1 (2003): 44–54.

Figure Credits

Fig. 1.1: Source: https://commons.wikimedia.org/wiki/File:Curtis%27s_Botanical_Magazine_Tab_9405_Aquilegia_grata_from_Karl_Maly%27s_sample_Dobrun_Bosnia_1909.JPG

Fig. 1.2: Source: https://commons.wikimedia.org/wiki/File:Phenylketonuria_testing.jpg

Fig. 1.3: Copyright © Wellcome Library (CC by 4.0) at https://wellcomeimages.org/.

Fig. 1.4: Copyright © (CC BY-SA 4.0) at https://cnx.org/contents/24nI-KJ8@24.18:NjE8d7G4@7/Mendels-Experiments.

Fig. 1.7: Source: https://commons.wikimedia.org/wiki/File:1905_Otto_Folin_in_biochemistry_lab_at_McLean_Hospital_byAHFolsom_Harvard.png

Fig. 1.7: Copyright © Cburnett (CC BY-SA 3.0) at https://commons.wikimedia.org/w/index.php?curid=1840082.

Fig. 1.9: Copyright © Spencer Baron (CC BY-SA 3.0) at https://commons.wikimedia.org/wiki/File:Incomplete_dominance.svg.

Fig. 1.9: Source: https://commons.wikimedia.org/wiki/File:ABO_blood_type.svg

Fig. 1.10: Source: https://commons.wikimedia.org/wiki/File:Dihybrid_cross.png

Chapter 2

Pedigrees and Probability: Applications to Human Genetics

It has been an amazing learning experience in Mendel's garden. So much to absorb—the Laws of Dominance, Segregation, and Independent Assortment. But what about human inheritance? We certainly can't do the types of genetic crosses and analyze hundreds of offspring per mating in humans! So—how do geneticists trace the patterns of inheritance in humans and make predictions on the chances of inheriting a genetic disorder? We will study the inheritance patterns of several human genetic disorders to answer this question.

Can We Predict Human Inheritance?

What Is Cystic Fibrosis?

Cystic fibrosis (CF) is an inherited recessive genetic disorder (see Figure 2.1). It is characterized by the production of a thick mucus in the lungs that results in serious breathing problems and recurrent lung infections that can ultimately result in death (see Figure 2.2). It is one of the most common recessive genetic disorders in Europe and the United States. Because it is a recessive disorder, both parents must be carriers for their child to inherit the disorder.

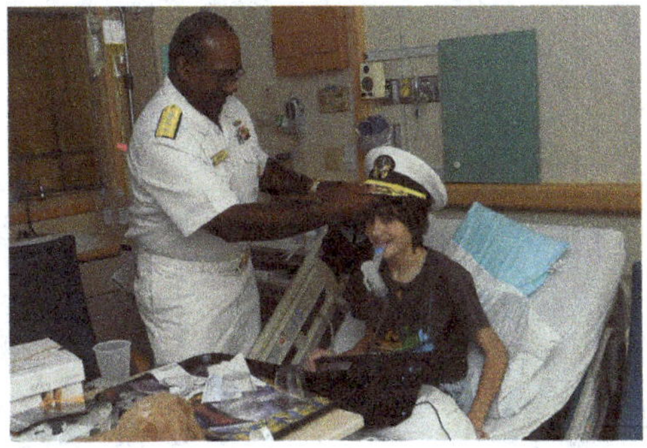

Figure 2.1

Girl receives gene therapy for cystic fibrosis

The Discovery of Cystic Fibrosis

In 1595 Professor Pieter Pauw (1564–1617) was the first to describe cystic fibrosis after examining a child who died of the disease. He wrote the following:

> *On January 16th 1595, I conducted an autopsy on an 11-year-old girl said to be bewitched. She had had strange symptoms for eight years. Inside the pericardium, the heart was floating in a poisonous liquid, sea green in colour. Death had been caused by the pancreas which was oddly swollen. It was very close to the rounded side of the liver, so that one could have thought, in touching it, that it was a scirrhous (a type of cancer with a hard and woody texture). When it was removed the interior was found to*

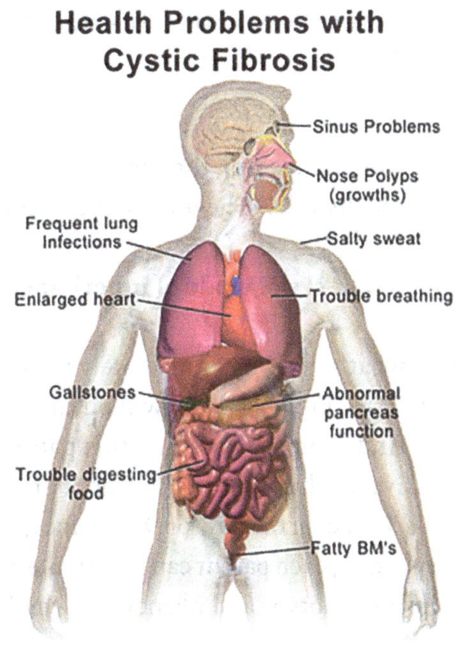

Figure 2.2

Health problems due to cystic fibrosis

be brightly coloured, a kind of hard white viscous mass. The little girl was very thin, worn out by hectic fever (a fluctuating) but persistent fever.

Little more was learned about the genetic origins of CF for the next several hundred years (see Figure 2.3). Then, in 1946, two scientists by the names of Dorothy Andersen and Richard Hodges carried out a study of more than 100 families and discovered that the disorder was hereditary and showed a recessive pattern of inheritance. They found that the incidence of CF in the siblings of children diagnosed with this disorder was approximately 25% (Andersen and Hodges, 1946).

Figure 2.3

Pieter Pauw performing an autopsy in the Anatomical Theatre in Leiden

Pedigree Analysis

To begin to learn more about this serious human disorder, we visit a genetics institute in New York City where researchers are studying children with CF. Dr. Andersen is examining a 3-year-old girl who shows signs of a disease called cystic fibrosis. He is taking a family history. Neither parent has the disorder; however, they are expecting another child and are worried that the baby will develop the same disorder. The doctor charts the family history in a diagram called a pedigree.

1. **What is the mode of inheritance of cystic fibrosis?**

Well, what strikes us immediately is that neither of the child's parents or any of the grandparents has CF (see Figure 2.4). How then can this be classified as an inherited disorder?

Dr. Andersen explains that this pattern is very common in inherited genetic disorders that are recessive. Each parent is a carrier of one normal allele and one defective allele that causes cystic fibrosis. Based on the Law of Dominance, heterozygotes show the dominant trait. Based on the Law of Segregation, each parent can contribute a recessive allele to the embryo at fertilization to produce the recessive genotype and phenotype, which in this case is the disorder cystic fibrosis (see Figure 2.5).

2. **What is the mode of inheritance shown in Figure 2.5?**

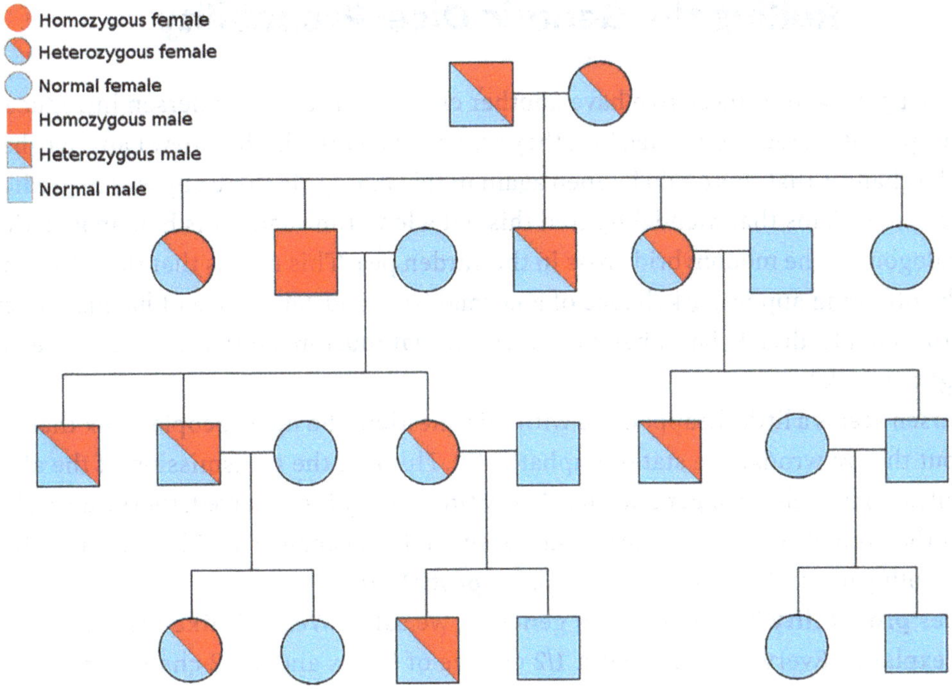

Figure 2.4

Pedigree analysis of human inheritance

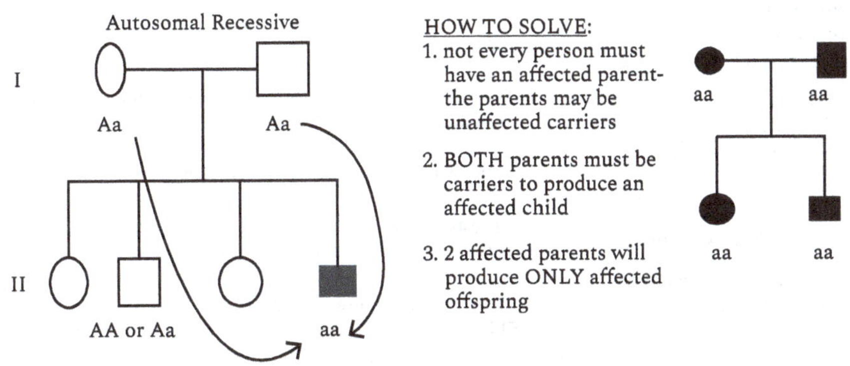

Figure 2.5

Tutorial on pedigree analysis: autosomal recessive inheritance

Rolling the Genetic Dice: Probability

Could this happen again if these two have another child, we ask? Dr. Andersen introduces us to the patient's parents, Greg and Emma. Yes, they are very concerned. Their new baby may have CF. What are the chances that this could happen again in this family? Is there any way to predict this?

Dr. Andersen explains that Mendel figured this out a long time ago! This human genetics situation is analogous to the monohybrid cross in the garden pea. This means that the 3:1 phenotypic ratio for the offspring applies: 3/4 chance of a normal baby and 1/4 chance of having a baby with CF. Well, this couple already has a baby with CF, so that must mean that the next three will be normal, right, we ask?

Dr. Andersen seems a little disappointed with this question. "So many people think that it works this way, but they're wrong!" he states emphatically. Think of the transmission of the abnormal recessive allele as the rolling of genetic dice. Every time a baby is conceived, there's a 3/4 chance it will inherit the normal allele from at least one parent and a 1/4 chance it will inherit the abnormal allele from both parents. It's based on the rules of **probability**.

What does **probability** have to do with genetics, we ask? "Well, it's like tossing a coin," Dr. Andersen explains. Every toss involves a 1/2 chance of heads and a 1/2 chance of tails. That's how probability works. There are two possible outcomes, but one cannot know ahead of time which result will occur when we toss the coin. That's why it's called probability—not "certainty" (see Figure 2.6).

Probability (p):

Think of the allele pair Aa as coins - heads for A and tails for a:

Toss a coin:

p heads = 1/2; p tails = 1/2

1943 Zinc Penny

So- when making gametes:

p (A) = 1/2; p (a) = 1/2

When gametes make a zygote = AA the zygote gets A from mom AND A from dad- so-multiply

p(A) × p(A) = 1/2 × 1/2 = 1/4

This is the PRODUCT Rule.

OK well, what if the zygote is 'aa'?

Same thing as tails-so

p(a) × p(a) = 1/2 × 1/2 = 1/4

And what about the zygote who gets A from mom and a from dad to become 'Aa'?

Same deal: p(A) × p(a) = 1/2 × 1/2 = 1/4

<u>But wait</u>! What if the zygote gets A from dad and a from mom? That could happen, too!

So-that means there's 2 ways to become 'Aa' zygote: EITHER you get A from mom and a from dad OR vice versa- so ADD the probabilities:

p(A)mom × p(a)dad = 1/2 × 1/2 = 1/4 OR

p(a)mom × p(A)dad = 1/2 × 1/2 = 1/4

So- 1/4 + 1/4 = 1/2 = the probability of zygote 'Aa'

This is the SUM Rule.

Figure 2.6

Tutorial on probability

It's hard to believe that the laws of inheritance are similar to a game of chance! But Dr. Andersen tells us that this goes back to the Entropy Law, that all matter is moving toward increasing randomness—and the uncertainty principle—that one can only estimate the positions and movements of atomic particles. "I'm sure Heisenberg could do a much better job of explaining this than I can. Maybe you should give him a visit." We decline politely. We're having enough trouble assimilating all these new principles of inheritance!

We go into Dr. Andersen's office where he explains the probability rules to us in greater detail. There are two general principles, the product rule and the sum rule.

The Genetics of Achondroplasia

Another patient family is coming in this afternoon. We decide to visit with them to learn more about probability and inheritance. This family history involves the inheritance of a genetic disorder called achondroplasia, a form of dwarfism. The parents both have the disorder and have just given birth to a son. Amazingly, the boy does not have this disorder. This is puzzling! If both parents have the disorder, then how can they have a child with normal growth? Dr. Andersen assures us—and the parents—that there is a logical explanation. First, he shows us the family history of achondroplasia (see Figure 2.7).

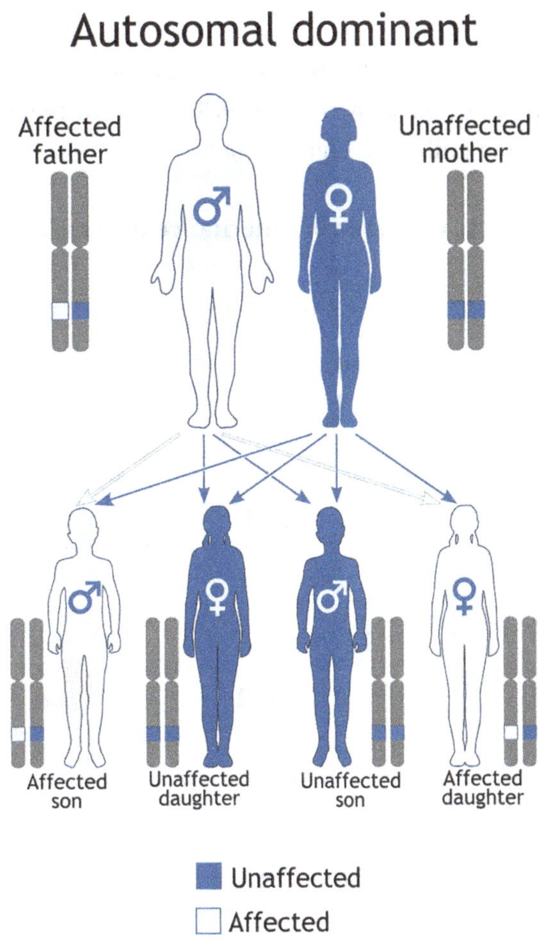

Figure 2.7

Inheritance pattern for achondroplasia-autosomal dominant

Then he explains that the pattern of inheritance for achondroplasia results from the fact that achondroplasia is an inherited dominant disorder (see Figure 2.8). Based on Mendel's Law of Dominance, this means that if you inherit only one defective allele that causes this form of dwarfism, you will have the disorder because heterozygotes show the dominant phenotype. To display normal growth, you need to inherit two copies of the normal allele. In this case, the recessive phenotype is "normal." Once again, the pattern of inheritance in this family can be explained by the monohybrid cross. Both parents are heterozygous for the dominant trait achondroplasia. But there

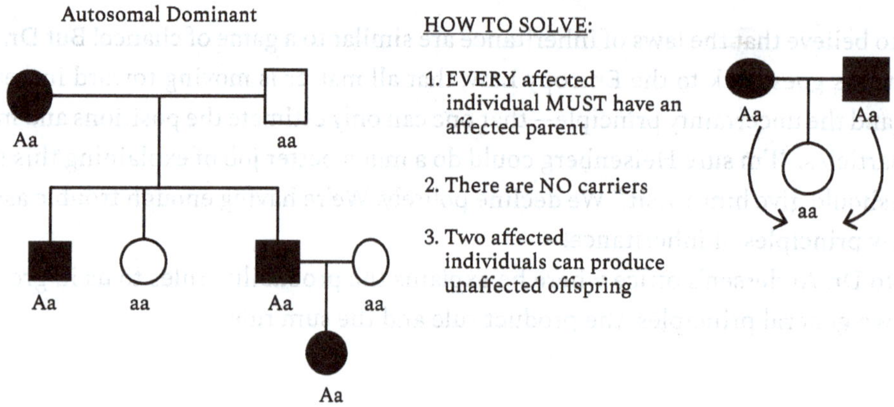

Figure 2.8

Tutorial on pedigree analysis:autosomal dominance

is a 1/4 chance that their baby could inherit the recessive allele from BOTH parents and. therefore, have normal growth pattern. This is how two parents with the genetic disorder can have an unaffected child (see Figure 2.9).

3. **Is the mode of inheritance the same as for achondroplasia? (See Figure 2.10.)**

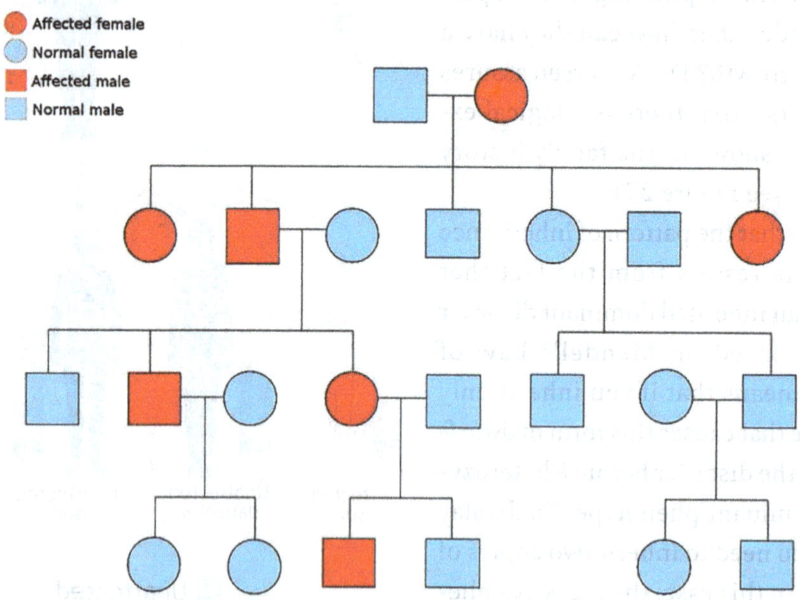

Figure 2.9

Pedigree of family with achondroplasia

Now we realize that whether an inherited disorder is dominant or recessive has a great effect on the pattern of inheritance and the probability that an inherited disorder can be transmitted from parents to their offspring.

What happens if only one parent has achondroplasia we ask? What is the probability that the baby will inherit the disorder? Well, that genetic cross would look like this, the doctor explains:

Aa X aa

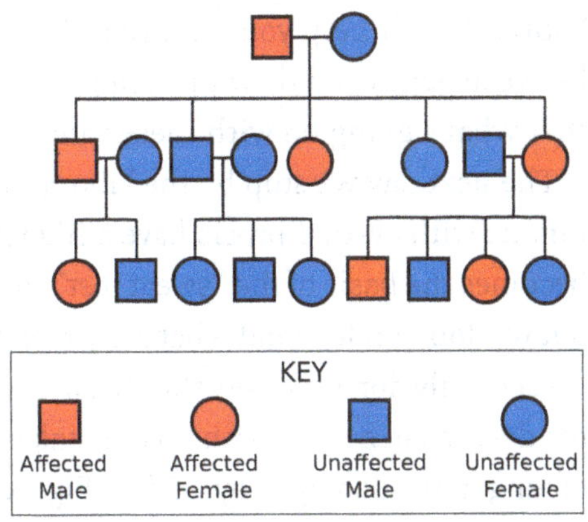

Figure 2.10

Unknown pedigree

The offspring will be 50:50: Aa = achondroplasia/aa = normal growth. That makes a lot of sense.

We spend the rest of the day helping Dr. Andersen calculate the probabilities of inheritance of genetic disorders in the families he is counseling.

4. **Amy and Paul both have achondroplasia, a bone-growth disorder that causes dwarfism. Achondroplasia is caused by an autosomal dominant allele. Individuals who inherit two copies of the allele do not survive to birth. Heterozygous individuals are dwarfs and recessive individuals have normal bone growth.**

   a. **What is Amy's genotype for the gene involved in achondroplasia?**
   b. **What is Paul's genotype for the same gene?**
   c. **What is the likelihood that they will give birth to a child with achondroplasia?**
   d. **What is the likelihood that they will give birth to a child without the condition?**

5. **You cross two true-breeding parents, one with purple flowers and one with white flowers, plant the seeds produced, grow the F1 generation an allow the plants to self-pollinate, and then count the number of offspring (the F2 generation) with purple and white flowers.**

   a. **If you counted 1,000 offspring and there was a 3:1 ratio of purple:white flowers, how many offspring would have purple flowers?**
   b. **How many would have white flowers?**

How Does Genotype Determine Phenotype?

By the end of the day, we are very tired; but we have one more question. Why is it that some disorders are inherited in a dominant fashion and others are recessive? Dr. Andersen shakes his head.

"Sorry, I can't help you with that. You'll have to talk to biochemists who study the relationship between genes and their protein products." We thank Dr. Andersen and resolve to investigate further what's going on with these inherited disorders.

The next day we stop by the laboratory of Dr. Paul di Sant'Agnese who, in 1953, discovered that infants with cystic fibrosis have a higher than normal level of salt in their sweat. This observation becomes the basis of the "sweat test" for CF in newborns. It sounds like a very important discovery, but we don't understand what salty sweat has to do with the lung damage that results from CF—and we certainly don't see how this discovery should tell us that this is a recessive disorder! We're hoping the doctor can help us with this. He takes us into his laboratory and shows us some microscope slides of lung tissue damaged by CF (see Figure 2.11). He then shows us a diagram to explain how this happens. As a result of the defective gene, ion channels in the lungs—and often in the pancreas—don't function properly altering the salt concentration in body fluids and causing the buildup of a thick mucus in the lungs that impairs normal function and causes infections that further damage lung tissue. That explains the biochemistry of the sweat test, but what about the recessive phenotype. Dr. di Sant'Agnese explains that individuals who are heterozygous—and have only one defective allele—are unaffected carriers of the disorder because their remaining normal allele produces enough receptor protein to allow the lungs to function normally. The disorder only manifests itself if there are no normal alleles in which case the receptor function is disabled—hence the recessive phenotype.

We are beginning to develop a deeper appreciation for the relationship between genotype and phenotype and how the proteins encoded by genes are responsible for the inheritance of dominant and recessive traits.

But what about achondroplasia? How can we account for its dominant phenotype?

To learn more, we visit the laboratory of Dr. John Wasmuth. Although the disorder has been documented since antiquity, it was not until 1994 that Dr. Wasmuth discovered the gene associated with the disorder, a growth factor receptor gene called fibroblast growth factor receptor. He shows us the research work he is doing to understand this form of dwarfism. He explains that achondroplasia is caused by a lack of growth hormone receptors needed for bone development. Individuals with only one normal copy of the gene—heterozygotes—show the disorder because their bodies produce only half the normal amount of receptor that is not sufficient to allow bones to develop normally. This is why achondroplasia has a dominant phenotype. This is very interesting!

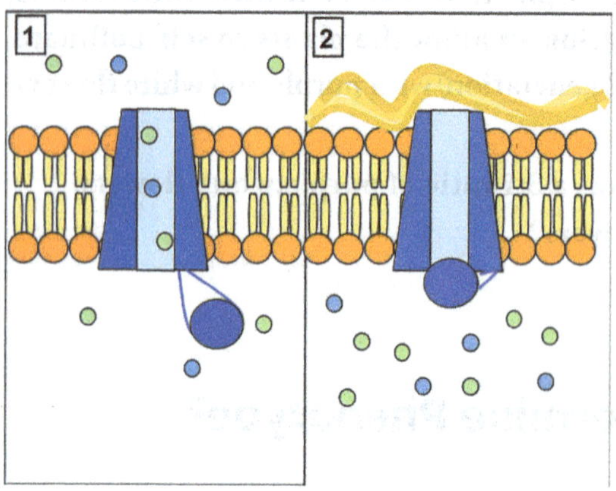

Figure 2.11

Biochemistry of cystic fibrosis

What about homozygotes who have no functional copy of the gene we ask? Dr. Wasmuth explains that this situation results in *in utero* death because the skeleton is so malformed. It becomes obvious to us that gene dosage, the number of copies of a gene, can be related to the amount of gene product produced—and this is a very important aspect of phenotype—determining whether the pattern of inheritance is dominant or recessive.

But what about incomplete dominance—remember the inheritance of flower color in 4 o'clock plants—are there any examples in human inheritance? To answer that question we visit Drs. Michael Brown and Joseph Goldstein at the Rockefeller University in New York City. They discovered the cholesterol receptor and found that in families with a rare genetic disorder called familial hypercholesterolemia (FH) the inheritance pattern is incomplete dominance. Individuals who are heterozygous—with one normal copy and one abnormal copy of the FH gene—have 1/2 the normal number of cholesterol receptors in their livers. This results in early onset—usually around age 40—of cardiovascular disease due to the buildup of cholesterol in their blood vessels. Individuals who have two defective alleles have a very severe form of atherosclerosis (onset in the twenties) due to a complete absence of this receptor. In the case of FH, the heterozygote has a phenotype in between the extremes of cholesterol metabolism—hence the mode of inheritance is incomplete dominance.

Accelerated lipid deposit rates dependent on whether individual is heterozygous or recessive (see Figure 2.12).

X-Linked Inheritance: Hemophilia

We are very impressed with the work of Brown and Goldstein—but we are anxious to learn more about the ways in which genes are inherited. There's something we've been curious about for a long time—why is it that some genetic disorders occur much more often in males than in females? Take hemophilia, for example.

We decide to visit the library to learn more about the history of this disorder. We learn that hemophilia is a clotting disorder that causes excessive and sometimes life-threatening bleeding from minor trauma. It was very prominent in the royal families of Europe, beginning with Queen Victoria, who apparently was a carrier of the disorder, although she did not suffer from hemophilia (see Figure 2.13). That means it was recessive. We also note that several of her sons were hemophiliacs, along with her grandsons, but none of her daughters or granddaughters.

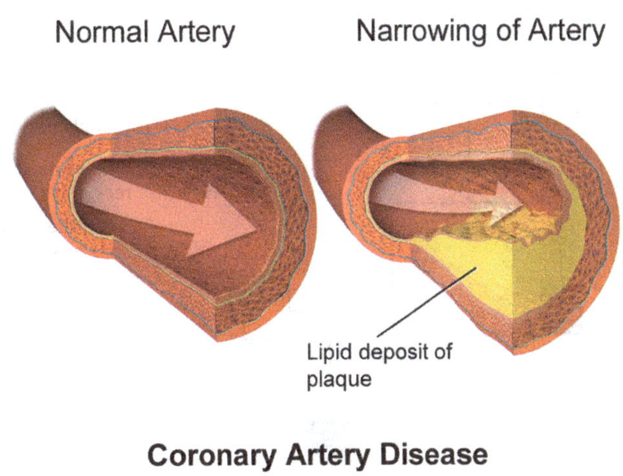

Figure 2.12

Human example of incomplete dominance

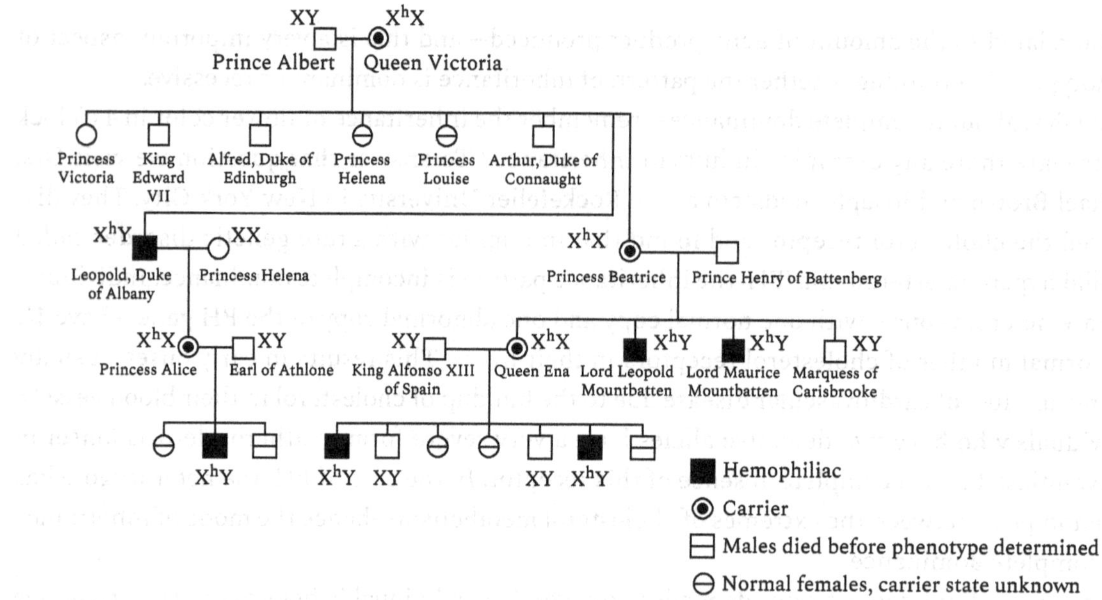

Figure 2.13

Pattern of transmission of X-linked gene for hemophilia in European royal family

What was responsible for this unusual pattern of inheritance? We learn that the gene is on the X chromosome. We need more information to understand what is going on here (see Figure 2.14).

We learn that genes are found on chromosomes—more on this later—and that there are two sex chromosomes that determine the gender of an individual, X and Y. All the other chromosomes are called autosomes to distinguish them from the sex chromosomes (see Figure 2.15). Females are XX

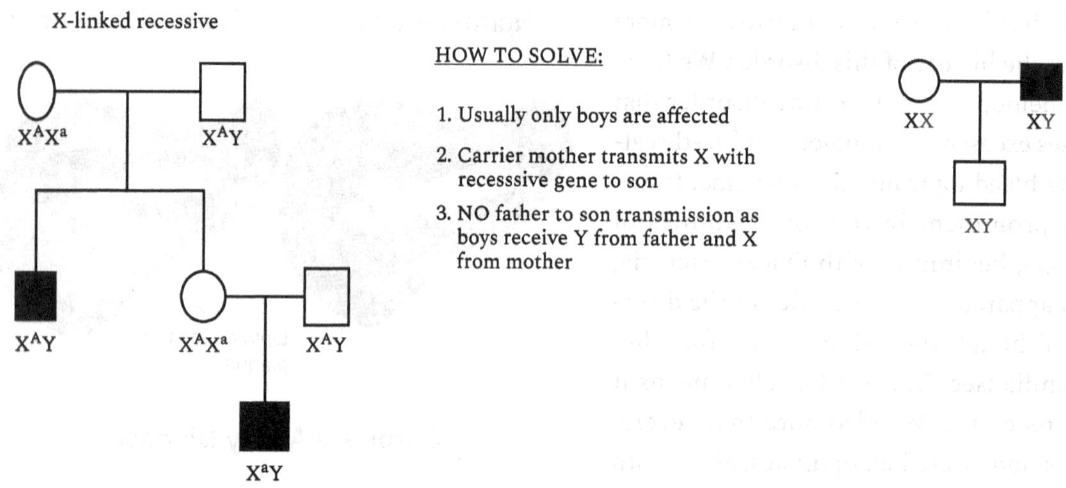

Figure 2.14

Tutorial on pedigree analysis: X-linked inheritance

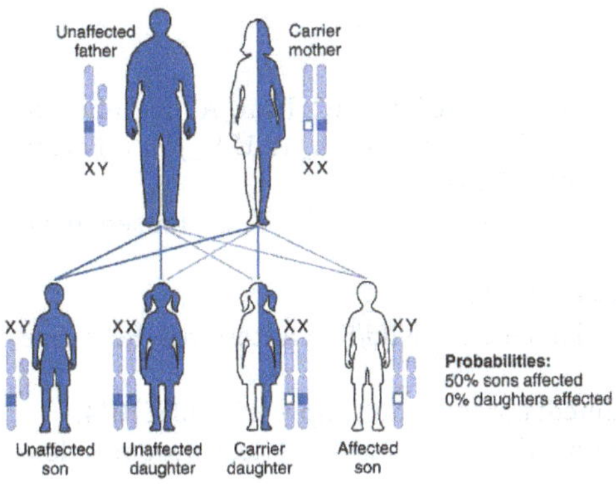

Figure 2.15

X-linked recessive inheritance

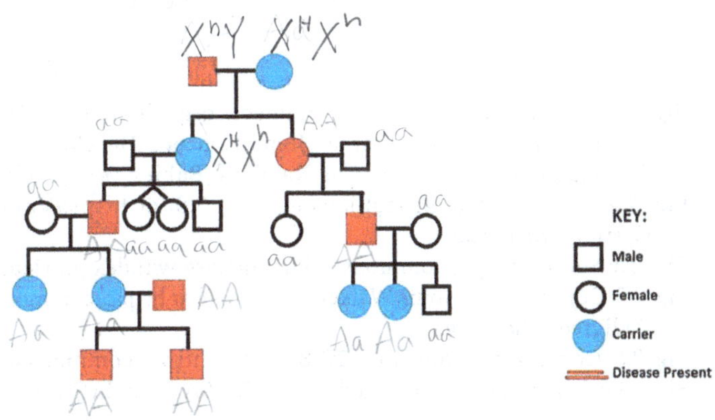

Figure 2.16

Unknown pedigree

and males are XY. The X and Y chromosomes for the most part, contain different genes. The Y chromosomes contains the genes that specify maleness. Therefore, for many genes on the X chromosome, females have two copies whereas males have only one copy because they only have one X chromosome. This has a great effect on determining patterns of inheritance that are different for males and females for the genes that are found on the X chromosome. Let's see how this works (see Figure 2.16).

6. **Is the first-generation female a carrier** (see **Figure 2.16**)? **How do you know?**
7. **Identify the genotype of each person in the pedigree** (**Figure 2.16**).

Summary

Here's what we've learned in this chapter:

- Autosomal versus X-linked modes of inheritance
- Sum rule and product rule in making genetics predictions
- Pedigree analysis: autosomal dominant and recessive, and X-linked recessive

There's so much important information that we decide to go to the library to research probabilities and pedigrees further.

References

Andersen, D. and Hodges, R. "Genetics of Cystic Fibrosis of the Pancreas With a Consideration of Etiology," *Am J Dis Child 72 no. 1. (1946): 62–80.*

Quinton, P. M., "Physiological Basis of Cystic Fibrosis: A Historical Perspective," *Physiological Review* 79, Suppl. 1 (1999): 3–22.

Figure Credits

Fig. 2.1: Source: https://commons.wikimedia.org/wiki/File:US_Navy_100901-N-6736S-002_Rear_Adm._Julius_S._Caesar,_right,_vice_director_of_Joint_Concept_Development_%5E_Experimentation_at_U.S._Joint_Forces_Command,_visits_a_patient_at_Rainbow_Babies_%5E_Children%27s_Hospital

Fig. 2.2: Copyright © BruceBlaus (CC BY 3.0) at https://commons.wikimedia.org/wiki/File:Blausen_0286_CysticFibrosis.png.

Fig. 2.3: Source: https://commons.wikimedia.org/w/index.php?curid=47278070

Fig. 2.5: Copyright © Jerome Walker (CC BY 3.0) at https://commons.wikimedia.org/wiki/File:Autosomal_Recessive_Pedigree_Chart.svg.

Fig. 2.8: Copyright © Domaina (CC BY 3.0) at https://commons.wikimedia.org/w/index.php?curid=18567014.

Fig. 2.11: Copyright © Simon Caulton (CC BY-SA 3.0) at https://commons.wikimedia.org/wiki/File:Autosomal_dominant.png.

Fig. 2.10: Copyright © Jerome Walker (CC BY 3.0) at https://commons.wikimedia.org/wiki/File:Autosomal_Dominant_Pedigree_Chart2.svg.

Fig. 2.12: Copyright © Lbudd14 (CC BY 3.0) at https://en.wikipedia.org/wiki/Cystic_fibrosis#/media/File:CFTR_Protein_Panels.svg.

Fig. 2.13: Copyright © BruceBlaus (CC BY 3.0) at https://commons.wikimedia.org/wiki/File:Blausen_0259_CoronaryArteryDisease_02.png.

Fig. 2.14: Copyright © C K Robinson (CC BY 4.0) at https://commons.wikimedia.org/wiki/File:Victoria_pedigree_Carriers.png.

Fig. 2.16: Copyright © OpenStax College (CC BY 3.0) at https://commons.wikimedia.org/wiki/File:2928_X-linked_Recessive_Inheritance-new.jpg.

Fig. 2.17: Copyright © Tangient LLC (CC BY-SA 3.0) at https://theworldwithoutcolour.wikispaces.com/Red-Green+Colour+Vision+Deficiency.

Chapter 3

Chromosomes and Inheritance

Learning about patterns of inheritance in humans using the tools of pedigree analysis and probability has been a fascinating experience. But we want to know more. Let's put away our pedigree charts and calculators for a while and go into the cell biology laboratory where we can begin to explore the cellular basis of inheritance: genes and chromosomes.

Down Syndrome

We are hurrying to England to the laboratory of Dr. John Langdon Down. He meets us at the doorway of a beautiful, large Victorian building and tells us that he has founded this hospital for children with developmental and intellectual disabilities. No sooner has he greeted us warmly than we are headed down a long corridor, a children's ward with beds on both sides with young children playing quietly together or just resting.

"I'd like you to meet two of my young friends," he says gently. He introduces us to two 4-year-old boys playing with building blocks. They look up at us at the same time and say "hi," smiling. "Twins?" we ask, admiring how cute they look. "No, that's what has puzzled me for such a long time," explains Dr. Down. "They're actually not related at all—they even come from different countries—yet they look alike! I've encountered many children like this and I find it puzzling that these children have the same features, similar disabilities, and yet are not genetically related." He looks up at us suddenly and asks pointedly, "What could be going on?"

For a moment we are concerned that he is looking to us for an answer—we have none—but then he adds reassuringly, "I think I figured it out! The reason they look alike even though they're not related is because the disorder itself is genetic—it's not inherited but must be due to the same genetic change in all of these unrelated individuals. They're alike because they share the same genetic difference!"

Wow—that seems amazing—the same genetic change in different, unrelated individuals. This means it's not inherited! "How could this happen?" we ask. Dr. Down looks downward. "I have no explanation for this. Maybe you should visit Dr. Flemming's lab. I hear he's studying cell bodies they are calling '**chromosomes**'—and he thinks they have something to do with genetics."

We thank Dr. Down, say good-bye to the boys and begin our trip to visit Dr. Walther Flemming. On our journey we learn from a fellow passenger that Dr. Down's own grandson, who was named after him, has recently been diagnosed with the disorder named for his grandfather (see Figure 3.1). We are extremely surprised to learn this and very anxious to discover what role chromosomes may play in this disorder.

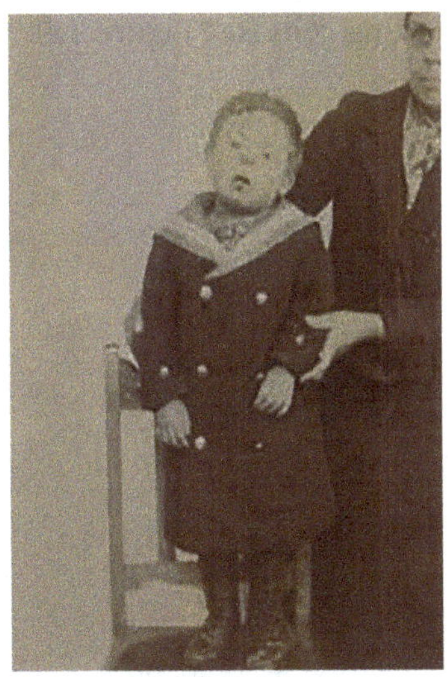

Figure 3.1

Photograph of Dr. John Langdon Down's grandson, his namesake, who had Down syndrome

The Discovery of Chromosomes

We enter the laboratory of Dr. Flemming, the founder of the field of cytogenetics—the study of the cellular basis of inheritance. Dr. Flemming is using aniline dyes to stain the cell nucleus. Under the microscope, he sees a mass of threadlike bodies that we now call **chromosomes**—which literally means "colored body" (see Figure 3.2).

The cells he is studying have very large chromosomes called "**polytene**" chromosomes that he is able to visualize with a light microscope. To his surprise, Flemming notices that the chromosomes begin to increase in number and then subsequently split apart as one cell divides in two. He terms this process "**mitosis**" (meaning thread) and begins to follow the pathway these unusual colored bodies take as they are passed from cell to cell. He invites us to take a closer look (see Figure 3.3).

Dr. Flemming opens his notebook and shows us drawings he has made of the movements and arrangements of chromosomes during the time when one cell divides to form two new cells. We ask to look under the microscope and Flemming shows us some very impressive images of dividing cells (see Figure 3.4).

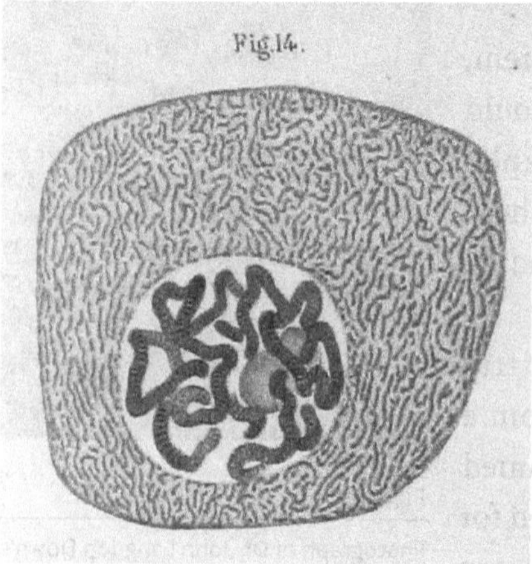

Figure 3.2

Polytene chromosomes from a salivary gland cell

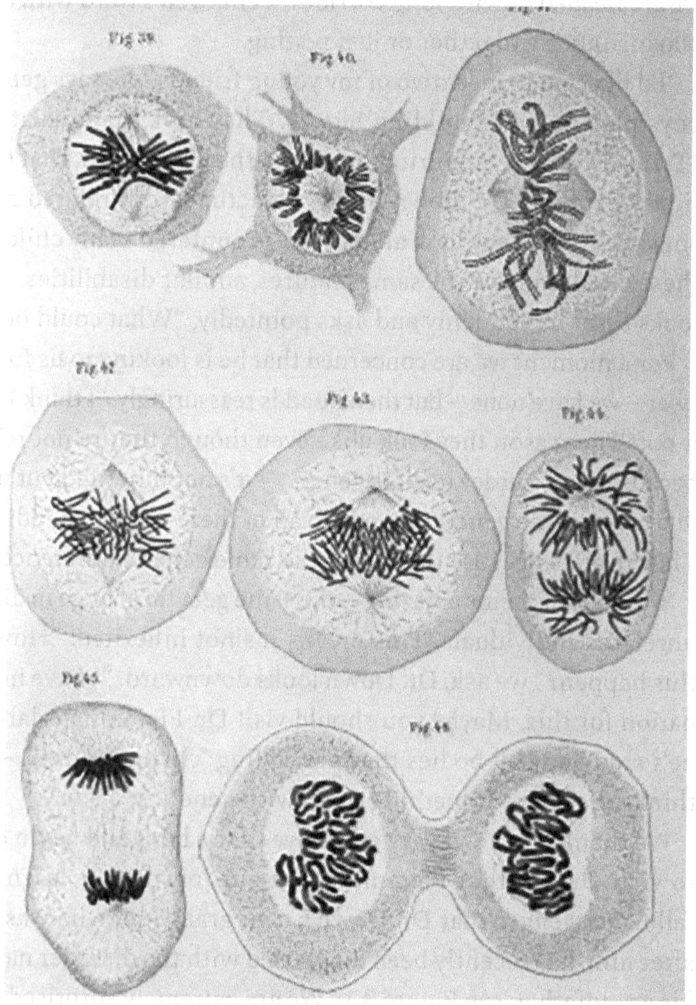

Figure 3.3

Flemming's drawings of chromosomes in dividing cells

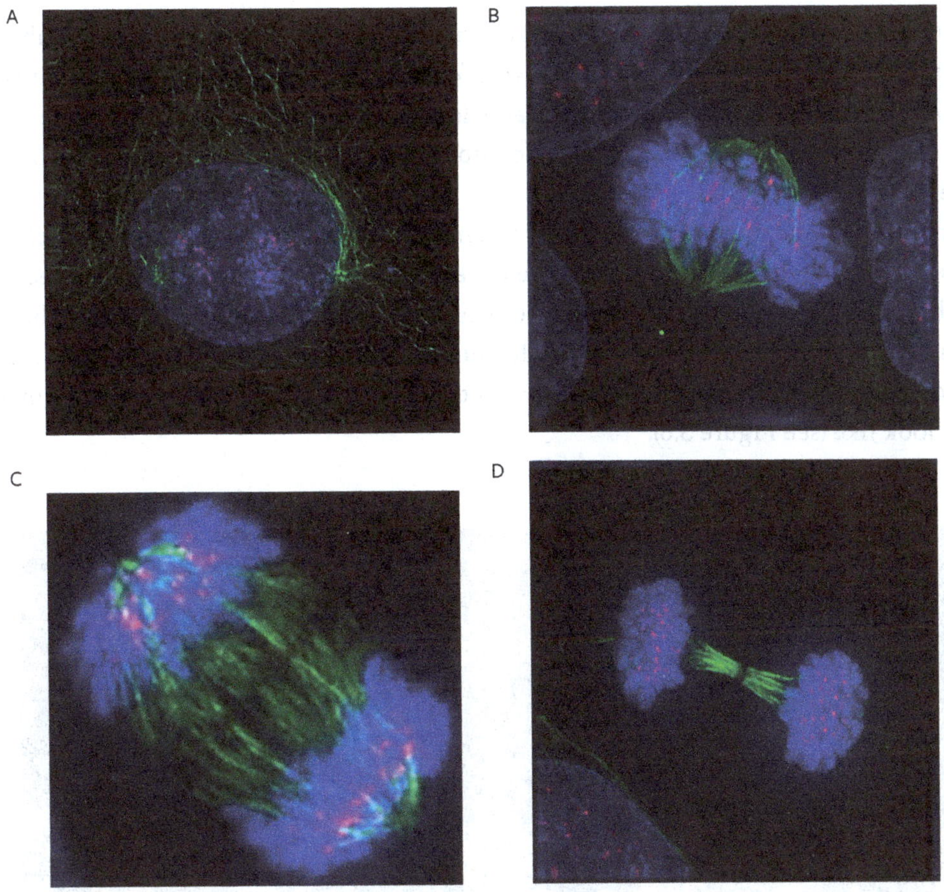

Figure 3.4

Photo of dividing cells

This is incredible! The chromosome movements look so highly orchestrated amid the dynamic restructuring of one cell to form two! We resolve to learn more about this amazing process!

Cells Divide to Form New Cells by Mitosis

Chromosomes are passed to new daughter cells during cell division, termed **mitosis.** Cells only divide when they receive a stimulus that sets in motion a series of events that begins with the duplication of each chromosome and ends with the completed process of cell division. The growth behavior of cells is defined as the **cell cycle**, a series of stages that characterizes the pattern of cell growth and division (see Figure 3.5). The portion of the cell cycle when cells are not dividing is called **interphase**.

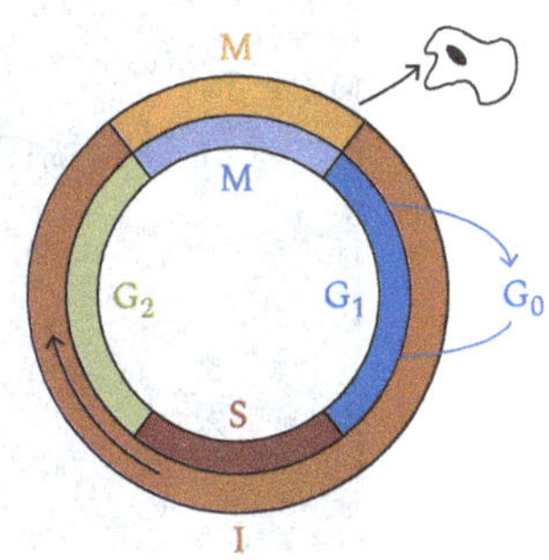

Figure 3.5

The cell cycle

We visit Dr. Theodore Boveri, one of the originators of the "Chromosome Theory of Inheritance." Boveri, unlike Flemming, knows about the work of Gregor Mendel, and realizes that the chromosome is the site where the genetic material is located. The genes that control inheritance are found on chromosomes that carry this genetic information as they are passed along from one cell to another.

The genotype defined by Mendel is actually a gene represented by two alleles on matching chromosomes. These matching chromosomes are called "**homologous chromosomes**" because they contain the same genes. One chromosome from each pair is inherited from your mother and the other is inherited from your father. This is why humans (and most other forms of life) are genetically diploid. Each cell of the body contains two sets of chromosomes. Let's see what human chromosomes look like (see Figure 3.6).

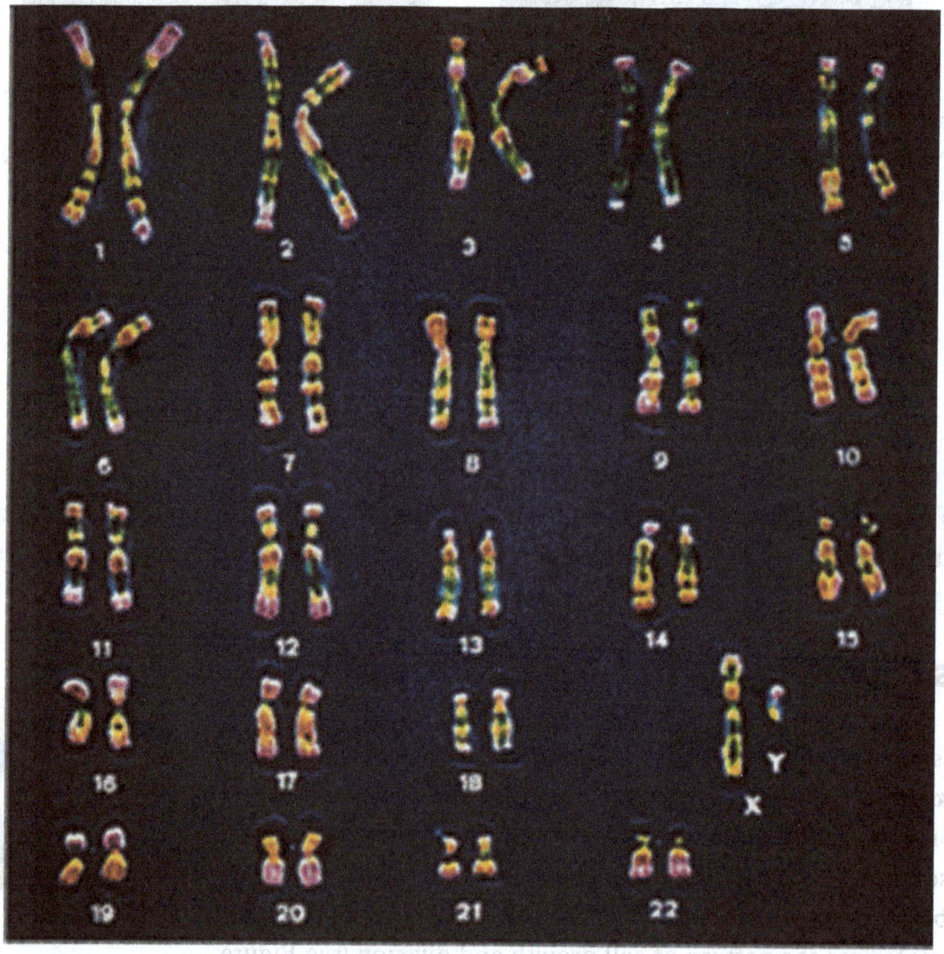

Figure 3.6

Chromosome painting: Human karyotype

The photo shows a "**karyotype,**" which is a chart prepared from human chromosomes that have been extracted from cells, stained, and the arranged in descending length order. We see that there are two copies of each chromosome. The total number is 46. This **karyotype** is from a male, because the last pair at the bottom of the chart, called the sex chromosomes, consist of a long X and a short Y set. Females have two copies of the X chromosome.

1. **What does it mean to be genetically diploid?**
2. **Why are the two chromosome copies called homologous?**
3. **True or false: Homologous chromosomes are identical.**

Let's take a closer look at a human karyotype (see Figure 3.7).

A closer look at chromosome 8 shows that it is divided into two segments called arms that are separated by a constriction called the centromere (see Figure 3.8). The shorter arm is called p and the longer arm is called q. By staining the chromosome with dyes, a unique pattern of bands is produced on each chromosome that allows them to be subdivided into regions and bands. This is an important tool for gene mapping. Using molecular methods to study genes and DNA, scientists have learned that about 8% of the genes on chromosome 8 are involved in brain development and about 15% are associated with cancer. If you compare chromosome 8 between humans and chimps,

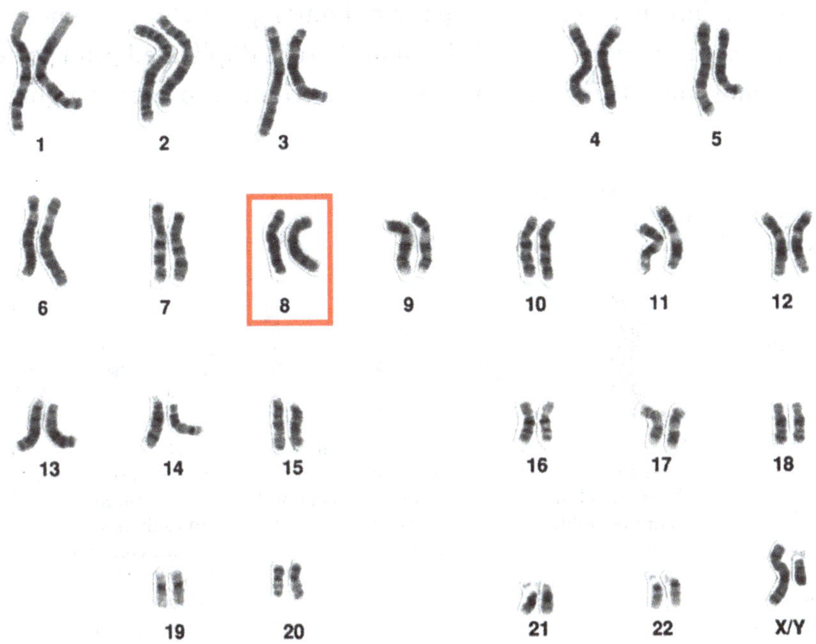

Figure 3.7

Human karyotype

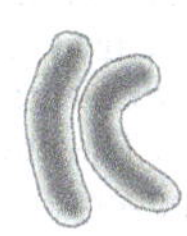

Figure 3.8

Chromosome 8

the genes involved in human brain development contain many differences from the same region of chromosome 8 of the chimp that may account to some extent for the large differences in brain function between the two species.

How Are Chromosomes Inherited?

We are fascinated by the idea that genes are located at specific sites along each chromosome and that's how they are transmitted from parents to offspring. But how are chromosomes inherited? We are directed to visit the laboratory of Dr. Walter Sutton who has been studying this question for many years. He is studying the chromosomes of grasshoppers and how they are inherited.

> *I may finally call attention to the probability that the association of paternal and maternal chromosomes in pairs and their subsequent separation during the reducing division ... may constitute the physical basis of the Mendelian law of heredity. (Sutton, 1902, 39)*

We want to learn more. Dr. Sutton has us take a look under the microscope to see what is happening. "I have proved Gregor Mendel's Law of Segregation and Independent Assortment," he boasts. Let me show you how it works (see Figure 3.9).

Let's see how this occurs in humans. We have 23 pairs of homologous chromosomes; therefore, the total chromosome count in humans is 46. Each of these is duplicated prior to cell division to produce 92 chromosomes. During mitosis 46 are distributed to each daughter cell,

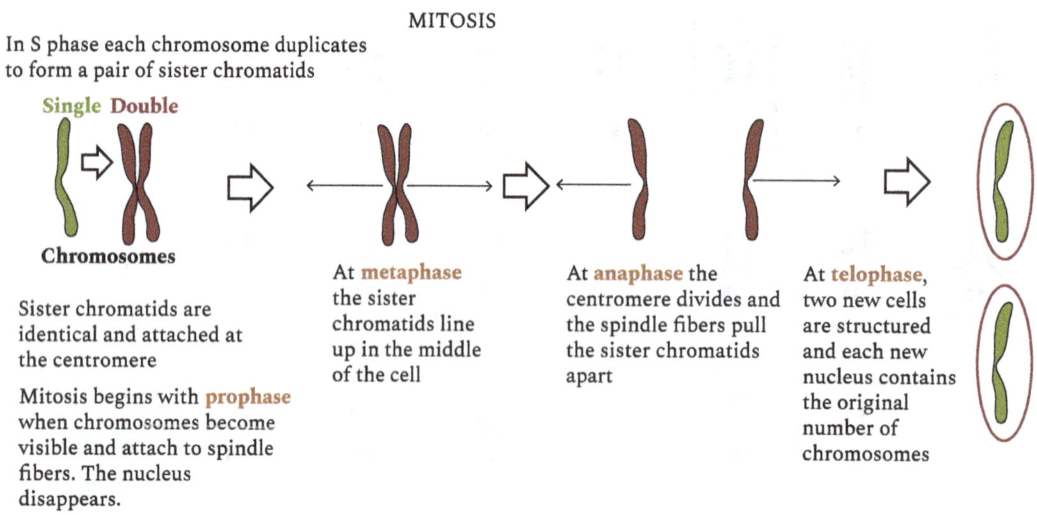

Figure 3.9

Tutorial: Mitosis

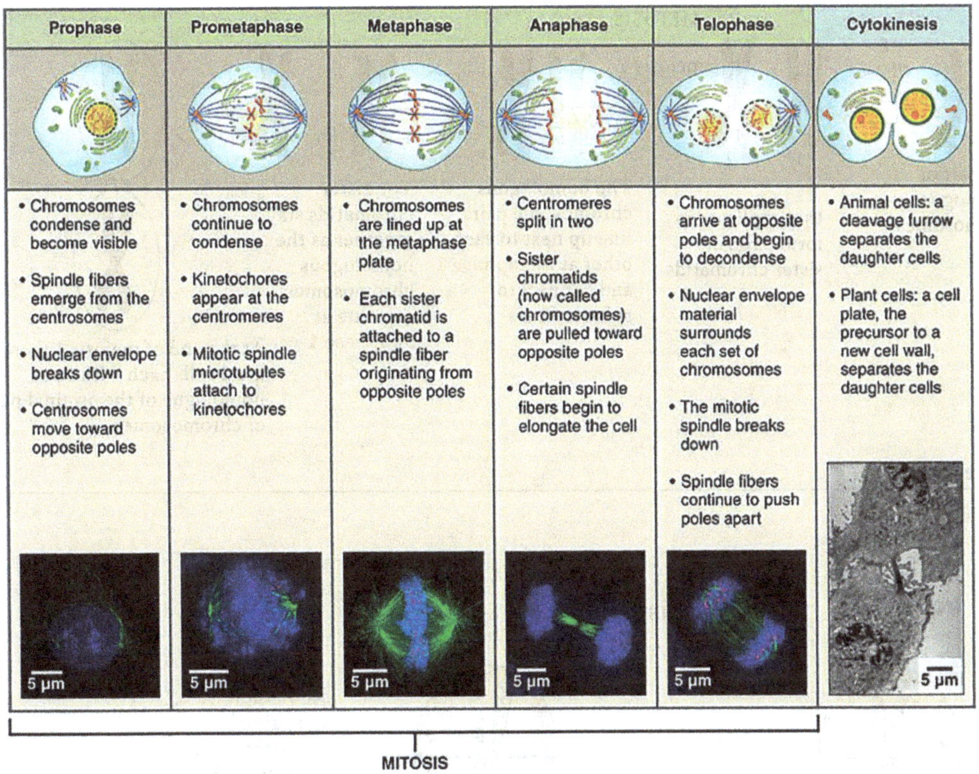

Figure 3.10

Mitosis in human cells

which ends up with 46. Let's look at dividing cells in each stage of **mitosis** (see Figure 3.10). In the process of cell division, the number of chromosomes remains the same in the parent and daughter cells.

Meiosis and the Production of Reproductive Cells

In each cell of your body one copy of every chromosome pair is inherited from your mother and the other copy is inherited from your father. The egg contains 23 and the sperm contains 23; when they fuse at fertilization, the fertilized egg and all its descendants have 46. How does this happen? We take a look at reproductive cells during the process of gamete formation. The distribution of chromosomes to produce gametes occurs by a specialized process of cell division called **meiosis**. Let's take a closer look at how this process occurs (see Figure 3.11).

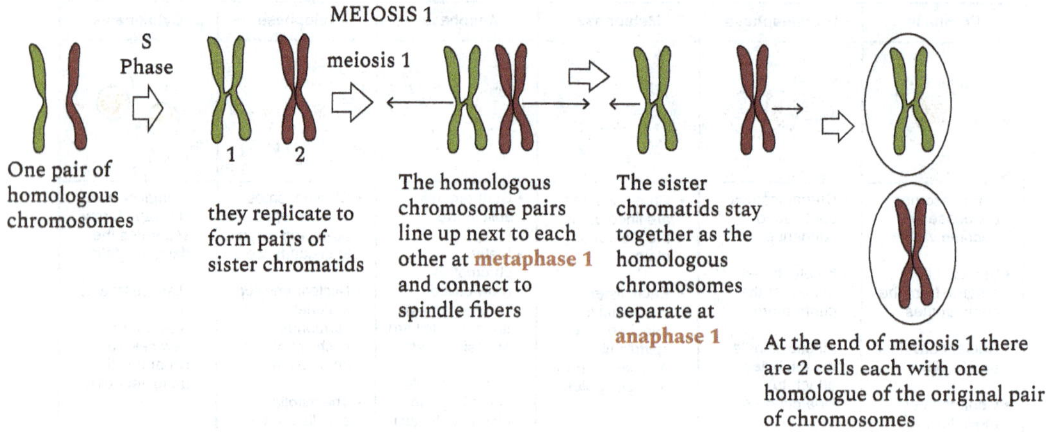

Figure 3.11A

Tutorial

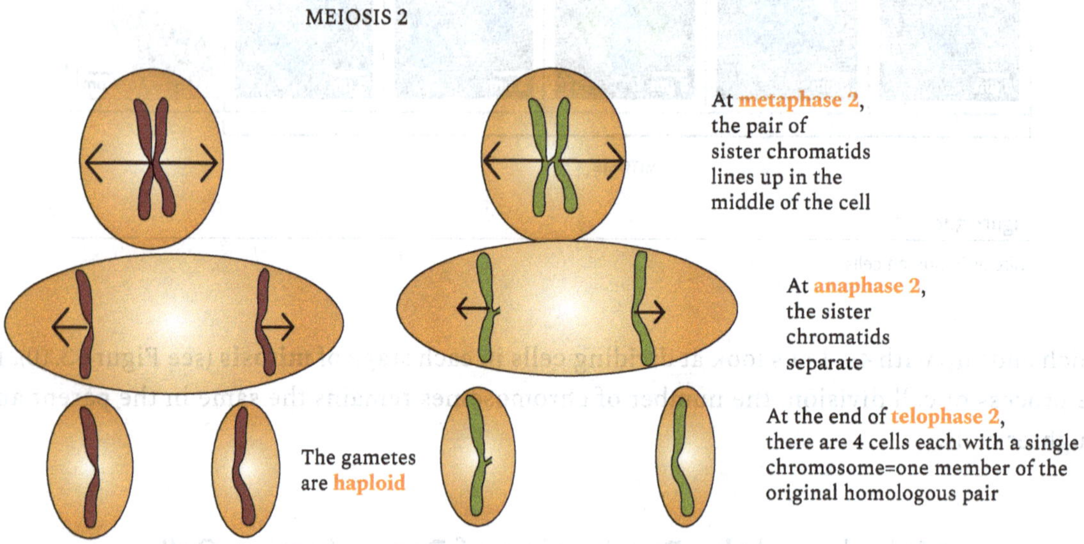

Figure 3.11B

Meiosis

We can see that a gamete contains only one copy of each pair of homologous chromosomes. The homologous chromosomes separate during anaphase of the first meiotic cell division. After the first division, the cell products contain each homologue as a pair of sister chromatids. The sister chromatids come apart during anaphase of the second meiotic division to produce **haploid** gametes.

Genetic Recombination

This is very impressive! An elaborate series of chromosomal movements generates haploid gametes—sperm and egg—that each contain only one set of chromosomes. Then Dr. Sutton tells us that something else truly remarkable happens during meiosis: The homologous chromosomes exchange segments in a process of recombination that shuffles all the alleles to produce a unique set on each chromosome. He shows us a diagram (see Figure 3.12).

In the original pink chromosome, A is inherited with b on the same chromosome. They are physically linked. But, after recombination, you could inherit a different allelic combination, A linked to B. Is this really true, we ask? Chromosomes can exchange pieces? How does that happen? The replicated homologous chromosomes—called a **tetrad**—connect with each other all along their length in a process called **synapsis**. The nonsister chromatids then exchange pieces by breaking off segments and reconnecting the pieces on the opposite chromatid. This is sometimes called breakage and reunion. It results in the exchange of alleles between homologous chromosomes.

Nondisjunction: An Error in Meiosis

The study of chromosomes has provided an explanation for how inheritance works—the precise distribution of genes and their alleles as cells move from one generation to the next by means of gamete formation and fertilization. But our studies of chromosomes and human karyotypes

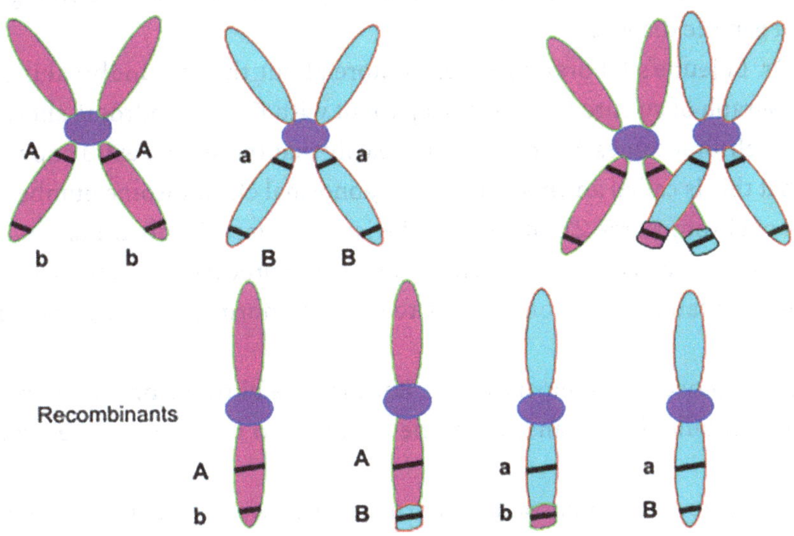

Figure 3.12

Genetic recombination

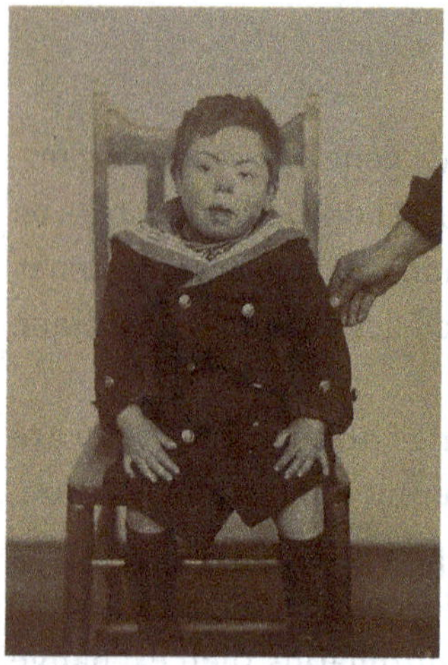

Figure 3.13

Photo: "Boy with Down Syndrome" St. Bartholomew's Hospital, England, 1908

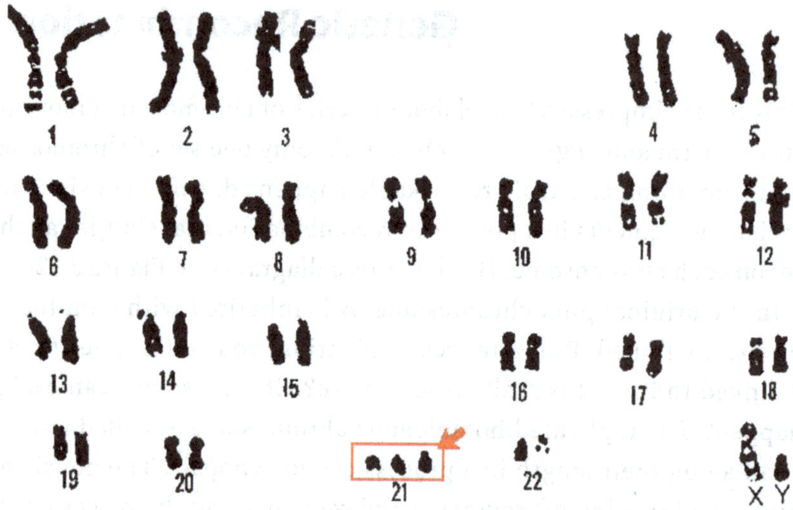

Figure 3.14

Karyotype of a boy with Down syndrome-trisomy 21

show that sometimes errors in meiosis occur—and they can have devastating consequences (see Figure 3.13).

As we saw earlier, Dr. Down started a hospital to care for children with this disorder, but little progress was made until 1959 when the French geneticist Jerome Lejeune discovered that a young boy with Down syndrome had an extra copy of chromosome number 21. He confirmed this finding in two other patients and this became the first time a specific chromosome change was shown to be the cause of a genetic disorder.

We hurry to Dr. Lejeune's laboratory to learn more about this groundbreaking discovery. He shows us a photograph of cultured cells from a patient with Down syndrome showing each of the numbered human chromosomes. We discern very easily that there is an extra copy of chromosome 21. He tells us that this is called an **aneuploidy**—or abnormal chromosome number. Because there are three copies of chromosome 21, this is called trisomy 21 (see Figure 3.14).

How can that happen we ask? We take a closer look at the process of meiosis to learn more about **nondisjunction**—the failure of chromosomes to separate normally during meiotic cell division (see Figure 3.15).

Nondisjunction can occur in meiosis 1 or 2. Because the chromosomes do not separate from each other as they should during anaphase, the gametes do not contain the proper number of chromosomes.

We will learn more about chromosomal abnormalities as we take a closer look at cytogenetics in the next chapter.

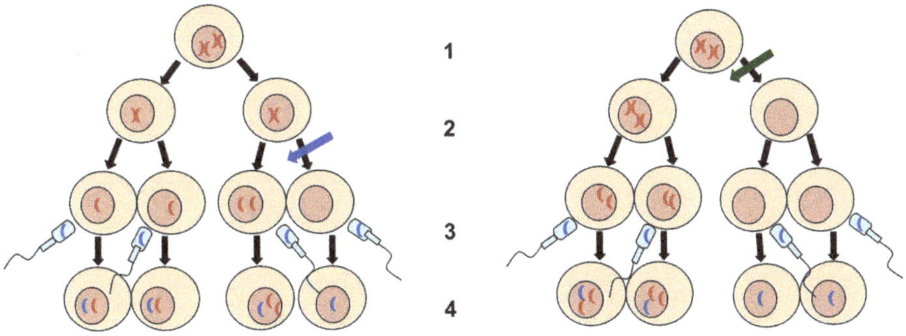

Figure 3.15

Nondisjunction

References

Ward, O., "John Langdon Down: The Man and the Message," *Down Syndrome Research and Practice* 6, no. 1 (1999): 19–24.

Sutton, Walter S., "The Chromosomes in Heredity," *Biological Bulletin*, no. 4 (1903): 231–251.

Figure Credits

Fig. 3.1: Copyright © St Bartholomew's Hospital Archives & Museum, Wellcome Images (CC BY 4.0) at https://commons.wikimedia.org/wiki/File:Boy_with_Down_syndrome_Wellcome_L0067016.jpg.

Fig. 3.2: Source: https://commons.wikimedia.org/w/index.php?curid=1251515

Fig. 3.3: Source: https://commons.wikimedia.org/wiki/File:Zellsubstanz-Kern-Kerntheilung.jpg

Fig. 3.4a: Source: https://commons.wikimedia.org/wiki/File:ProphaseIF.jpg

Fig. 3.4b: Source: https://commons.wikimedia.org/wiki/File:MetaphaseIF.jpg

Fig. 3.4c: Source: https://commons.wikimedia.org/wiki/File:Anaphase_IF.jpg

Fig. 3.4d: Source: https://commons.wikimedia.org/wiki/File:TelophaseIF.jpg

Fig. 3.5: Copyright © Magnus Manske (CC BY-SA 3.0) at https://commons.wikimedia.org/wiki/File:Cell_cycle.png.

Fig. 3.6: Source: http://www.nurkopedia.pl/index.php/Plik:Chromosom_kariotyp.gif

Fig. 3.7: Source: https://commons.wikimedia.org/wiki/File:Human_male_karyotpe_high_resolution_-_Chromosome_8.png

Fig. 3.8: Source: https://commons.wikimedia.org/wiki/File:Human_male_karyotpe_high_resolution_-_Chromosome_8.png

Fig. 3.10: Copyright © OpenStax (CC BY 4.0) at https://cnx.org/contents/1tJ55Ot6@7/The-Cell-Cycle.

Fig. 3.12: Copyright © Abbyprovenzano (CC BY 3.0) at https://commons.wikimedia.org/wiki/File:Chromosomal_Crossover.svg.

Fig. 3.13: Source: https://wellcomecollection.org/works/rd2r9gbh?query=%E2%80%9CBoy+with+Down+Syndrome%E2%80%9D+St.+Bartholomew%E2%80%99s+Hospital%2C+England%2C+1908

Fig. 3.14: Source: https://commons.wikimedia.org/wiki/File:21_trisomy_-_Down_syndrome.png

Fig. 3.15: Copyright © Tweety207 (CC BY 3.0) at https://commons.wikimedia.org/wiki/File:Nondisjunction_Diagrams.svg.

Chapter 4

Cytogenetics

Leukemia: What Do Chromosomes Have to Do with It?

Almost 50 years ago, David Hungerford and I noticed an abnormally small chromosome in cells from patients with chronic myelogenous leukemia (CML). Our observation that all the neoplastic cells in nearly all cases of a specific human cancer contained a consistent somatic genetic change provided strong evidence to support Boveri's hypothesis that a critical genetic alteration in a single cell, which provided the cell with a growth advantage, could give rise to a tumor. (Nowell, 2007)

We are so excited to learn more about chromosomes that our (loud) conversation is overheard by a young girl standing nearby on the train station platform. "I'm on my way to Philadelphia to learn all about MY chromosomes," she states excitedly. "Would you like to come along?" Her family encourages us to join them and before we know it we are inside a large city hospital heading for the office of Dr. Peter Nowell. He greets the family warmly and we are all ushered inside.

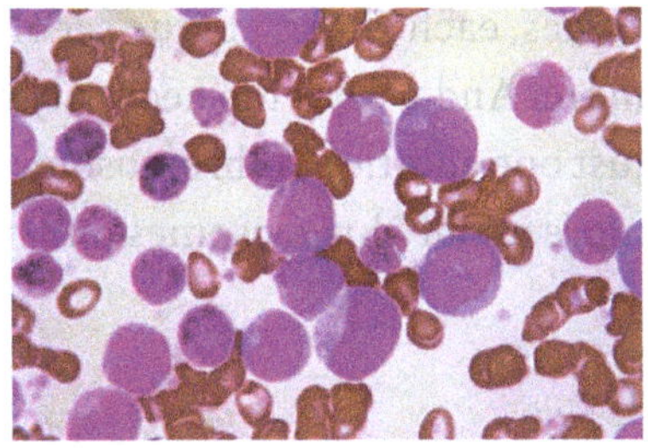

Figure 4.1

Chronic myeloid leukemia cells

"I invited you to come to our hospital so I could test your chromosomes," he says comfortingly. "I have recently observed that several people with the type of leukemia you have been diagnosed with all have the same chromosomal abnormality. If your chromosomes show the same difference, this will go a long way toward proving that abnormal chromosomes can cause cancer as Boveri has proposed."

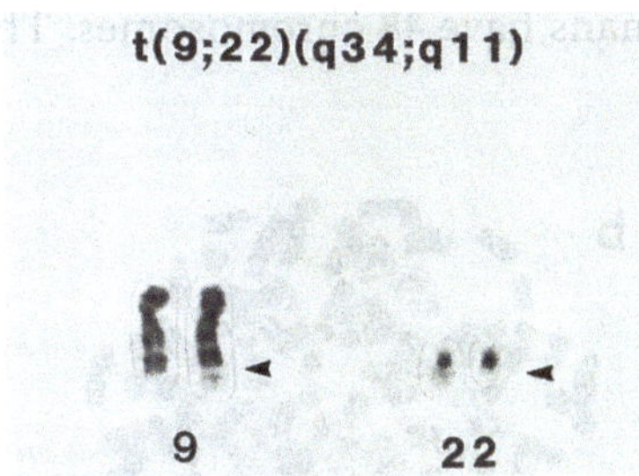

Figure 4.2

The Philadelphia chromosome

The young girl's blood is drawn and we view the cells under the microscope. We see the large number of red myeloid cells that are characteristic of this type of leukemia (see Figure 4.1).

Next, Dr. Nowell prepares a chromosome spread from the blood cells and takes a look under the microscope. "There it is!" He exclaims. "Take a look!" (See Figure 4.2.)

We rush to take turns peering into the bright lights of the oculars, while Dr. Nowell guides our focus to chromosome 22—it is shorter than normal. "That confirms my diagnosis!" he states excitedly. "This type of leukemia must be caused by an abnormality of chromosome 22. We'll call it the Philadelphia chromosome." We are amazed to learn that a single chromosome change can cause leukemia. "Now that we have identified a chromosomal change linked to this disease, this is the first step to finding an effective treatment," explains Dr. Nowell reassuringly (see Figure 4.3).

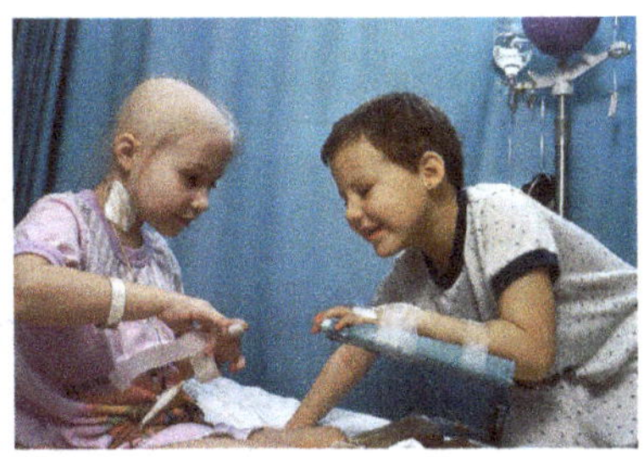

Figure 4.3

Children with leukemia receive chemotherapy treatment

We are all very pleased and relieved to learn this. But Dr. Nowell's observations have raised more questions than answers. How can a chromosome change cause cancer? And what caused this chromosome defect?

Dr. Nowell refers us to the laboratory of Dr. Tjio. "He'll explain it to you—he knows a lot more about chromosomes than I do!"

Our studies of chromosomes have shown how genes are packaged and delivered from cell to cell. We are struck by the precision required to ensure that the appropriate number and types of chromosomes are delivered to new cells during cell division. Just think, 23 pairs of human chromosomes, each with a unique set of genes, each gene represented by exactly two copies—no less—no more! And we see the necessity for this precision—if **nondisjunction** occurs and the cell receives just one additional chromosome—serious genetic disorders can result. We decide we want to learn more about chromosomes and how they are studied.

Karyotype Analysis

We are invited to visit the lab of Dr. Tjio who has been studying human chromosomes for many years. "Can you believe it?" he asks. "For the past 30 years, everybody has been thinking that humans have 48 chromosomes. That's ridiculous! I have just discovered a new method of studying chromosomes that shows that there are actually 46 human chromosomes! Would you like to see?" We are intrigued—how could so many people be so wrong? And just how did Dr. Tjio find the correct number?

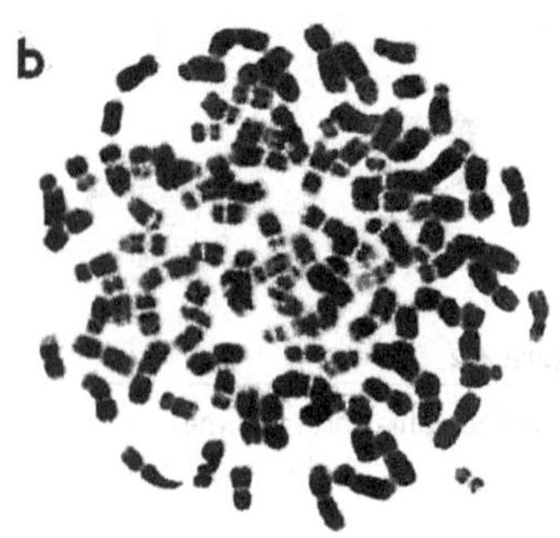

Figure 4.4

Chromosome spread

He tells us the method is called **karyotype analysis**. He takes human cells and grows them in culture. When they are all dividing—in the M stage of the cell cycle—he freezes the process by adding a drug called colchicine. This drug paralyzes the mitotic spindle fibers required to separate the chromosomes during mitosis—all the cells arrest in mitosis when the chromosomes can be easily seen under the microscope. Dr. Tjio shows us some of his photographs. "This is a mitotic spread showing the chromosomes as they look under the microscope," he states proudly (see Figure 4.4).

1. **Why is it necessary to freeze the cell cycle during mitosis to visualize the individual chromosomes?**

He then extracts the chromosomes from the cells and puts them in water—this causes them to swell so that they can be seen more easily. Then he stains the chromosomes with a dye called Giemsa that bonds to the nucleic acid and photographs them while they are under the microscope.

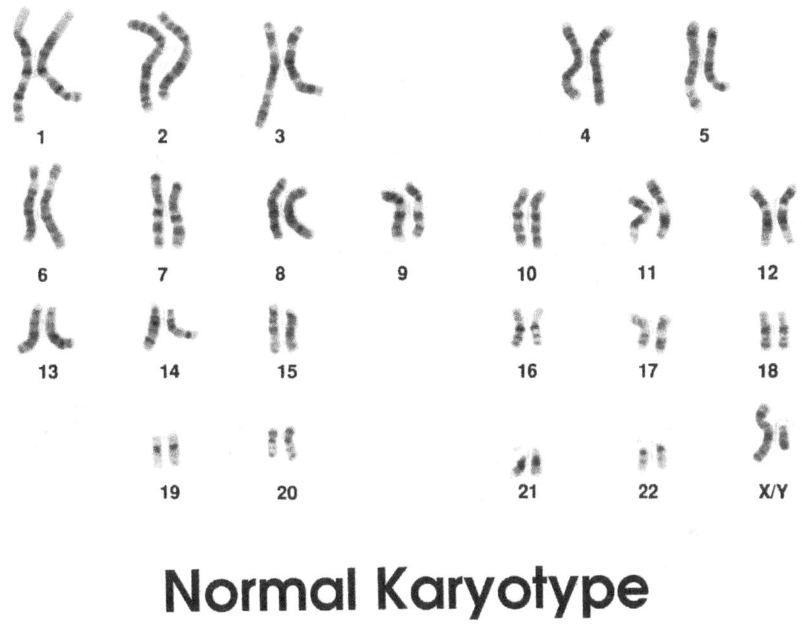

Figure 4.5

Normal human karyotype

After this, he arranges the chromosomes in pairs by cutting and pasting to produce a **karyotype** (see Figure 4.5). All the chromosomes are arranged in pairs.

2. **Why are the chromosomes arranged in pairs in a karyotype?**
3. **Why does each chromosome have an attached partner?**

Aneuploidies

We can easily see that there are 46 chromosomes. Dr. Tjio explains that this method of **karyotype** preparation has allowed geneticists to learn a lot more about chromosome structure and function and the chromosomal basis of many genetic disorders. For example, if the karyotype shows an **aneuploidy**, an abnormal number of chromosomes, we can figure out which chromosomes are involved. We remember our study of Down syndrome and that this disorder results from an extra copy of chromosome 21 (see Chapter 3).

Dr. Tjio tells us that there are other chromosomal **aneuploidies** that have been identified since then. We go into the lab to take a closer look. We look under the microscope and immediately see that there is an extra copy of chromosome 13 (see Figure 4.6).

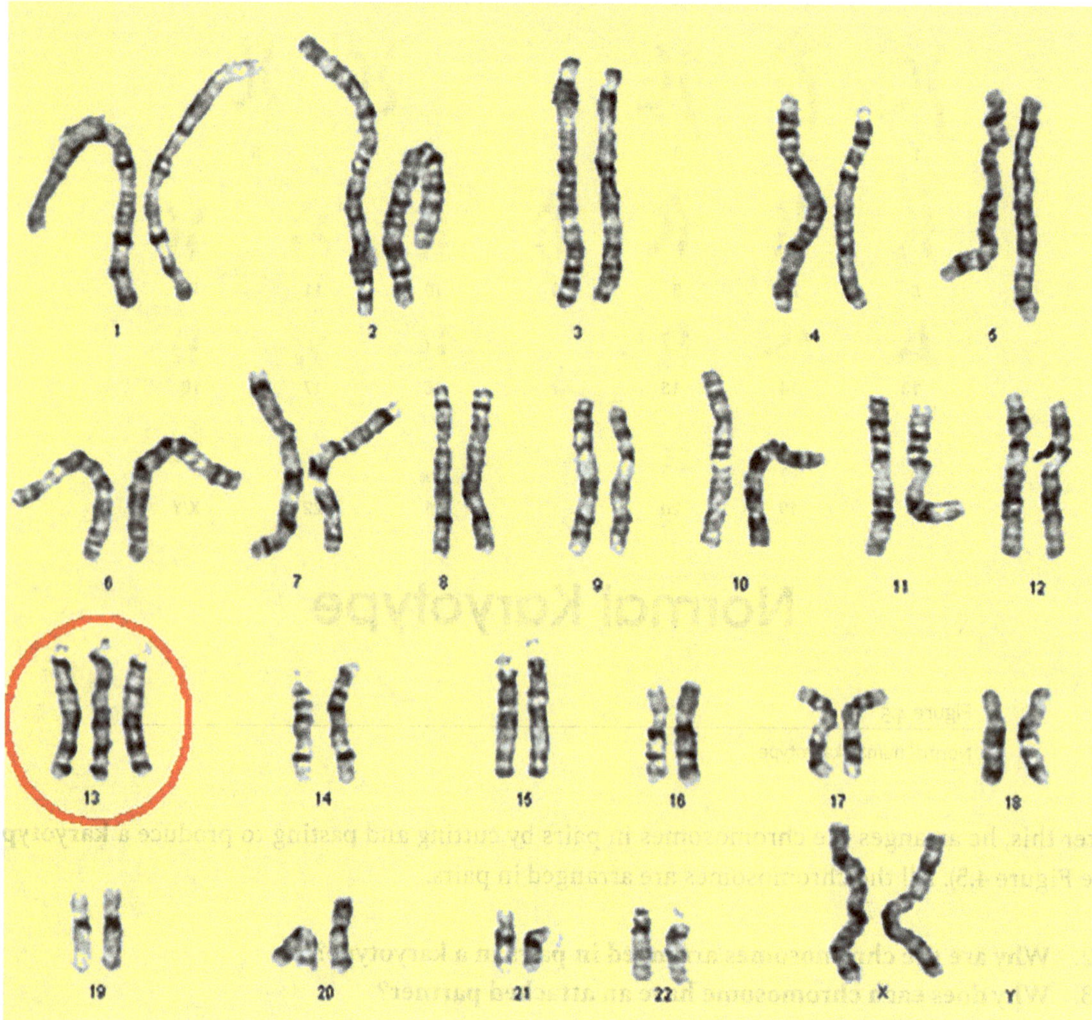

Figure 4.6

Karyotype showing trisomy 13, Patau syndrome

"This is a disorder called Patau syndrome," he tells us. "It results from **nondisjunction** as we saw in Down's syndrome—but a different chromosome—number 13—is present in triplicate, which causes a more severe genetic disorder. There is very little brain development, and infants born with this very rare disorder usually die in infancy." Dr. Tjio has been preparing karyotypes from miscarried fetuses and has determined that **trisomies** (three copies) of every autosome can occur and most **autosomal trisomies** result in death in utero. We begin to understand the importance of chromosome number—even one extra copy can be lethal.

The sex chromosomes are different, he says. There are several types of sex chromosome **aneuploidies** that occur for the X and Y chromosome that do not have as serious consequences as the

autosomal aneuploidies. Let's take a look at a summary of the most common human aneuploidies and what causes them (see Figure 4.7).

X Chromosome Inactivation

We learn that sex chromosome aneuploidies are more common and less serious generally than autosomal aneuploidies. We've looked at the X chromosome before. We want to learn more about the sex chromosomes. We visit the laboratory of Dr. Murray Barr who invites us in to look at an exciting finding he has just made. "If you look at cells from females under the microscope," he tells us, "you will see a dark spot in the nucleus—this is called the **Barr body**—I named it after myself!' he says triumphantly. "Well, what is it?" we ask. "It's a condensed inactive X chromosome. Females inherit one copy of X from their mothers and one copy from their fathers. At about the 8th week of embryogenesis, one copy of X—either the maternal or paternal copy—is targeted for condensation and inactivation." This process is called **lyonization**—after Dr. Mary Lyons—who named it after herself. All these names are getting confusing, but we are very interested nevertheless. This means that each female cell really has only one functional X chromosome, just like males (see Figure 4.8).

ANEUPLOIDY	KARYOTYPE	FREQUENCY
AUTOSOMAL		
TRISOMY 21 (DOWN SYNDROME)	47, XX or XY, +21	1/700
TRISOMY 13 (PATAU SYNDROME)	47, XX or XY, +13	1/5000
TRISOMY 18 (EDWARD SYNDROME	47, XXor XY, +18	1/10000
SEX CHROMOSOME		
MONOSOMY X, TURNER	45, XO (FEMALE)	1/5000
TRISOMY X	47, XXX (FEMALE)	1/700
TRISOMY XY, KLEINFELTER	47, XXY (MALE)	1/500
TRISOMY YY	47, XYY (MALE)	1/10000

Figure 4.7

Chart showing human aneuploidies

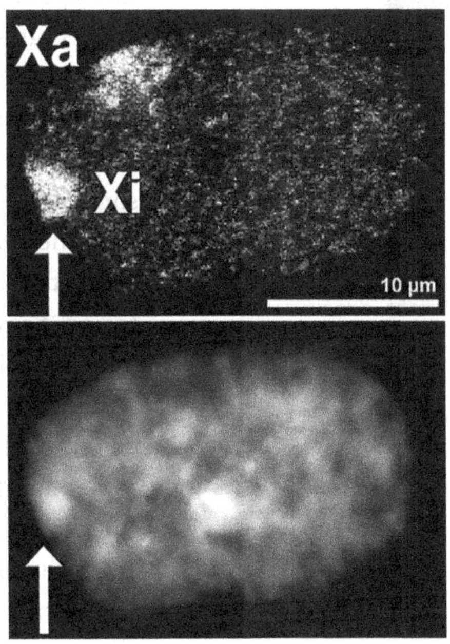

Figure 4.8

X chromosome Barr body

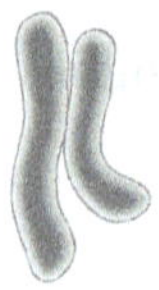

Figure 4.9

Chromosome 5 deletion responsible for cri du chat syndrome

Chromosome Structure Abnormalities

Dr. Barr shows us some chromosome preparations from other patients. "Are these more aneuploidies"?" we ask. "No. These patients have the normal number of chromosomes, 46, but there are other structural issues with one or more of their chromosomes."

We look at another microscope slide and at first it appears normal until we notice that one copy of chromosome 5 is slightly shorter than the other.

"What happened here?" we ask. "Well, for reasons that are not very well understood, some children have this chromosome abnormality—a missing piece from chromosome 5," Dr. Barr explains. "This is called a **deletion**. It results in a genetic disorder called cri du chat, meaning 'cry of the cat,' after the sound of the newborn's cry—like meowing—when this disorder is present. It results in a very severe developmental and cognitive impairments" (see Figure 4.9).

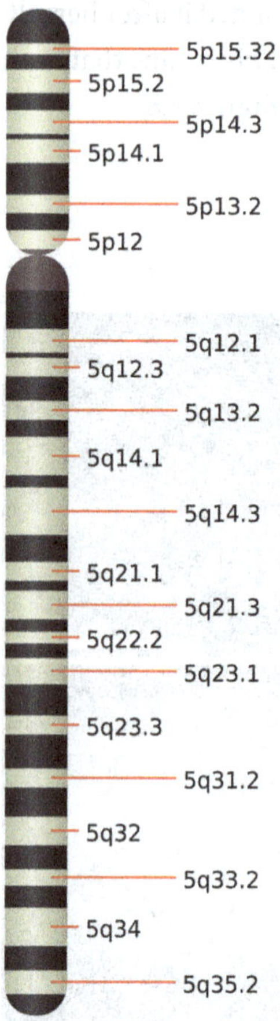

Figure 4.10

Diagram of chromosome 5

We don't understand how such a small change in chromosome structure can have such dramatic effects on biological function. We decide to take a closer look at the structure and organization of chromosomes. Each chromosome is like a string of beads, where each bead represents a gene. When chromosome rearrangements occur this changes genes by removing some or adding extra copies—or even sending them to a different chromosomal location. Often chromosome rearrangements involve many genes that are rearranged at the same time as a large chromosome piece is affected. Let's take a closer look at chromosome 5, which is involved in cri du chat syndrome (see Figure 4.10).

This disorder is caused by the **deletion** of the top of the short arm of chromosome 5, usually in the paternally derived copy of this chromosome, for reasons that are unknown. The deleted portion of this chromosome contains two critical regions responsible for the physiological characteristics of this disorder. Two genes have been identified in this region, **Semaphorine F and Delta catenin**, which appear to be required for normal brain development.

Studying the cri du chat deletion syndrome has greatly increased our understanding that genes occupy fixed locations on specific chromosomes and that the loss of even one copy of a gene can have profound consequences on development.

Another **deletion syndrome**, called DiGeorge syndrome, results from an internal deletion of a chromosome segment from the long arm of chromosome 22 (see Figure 4.11).

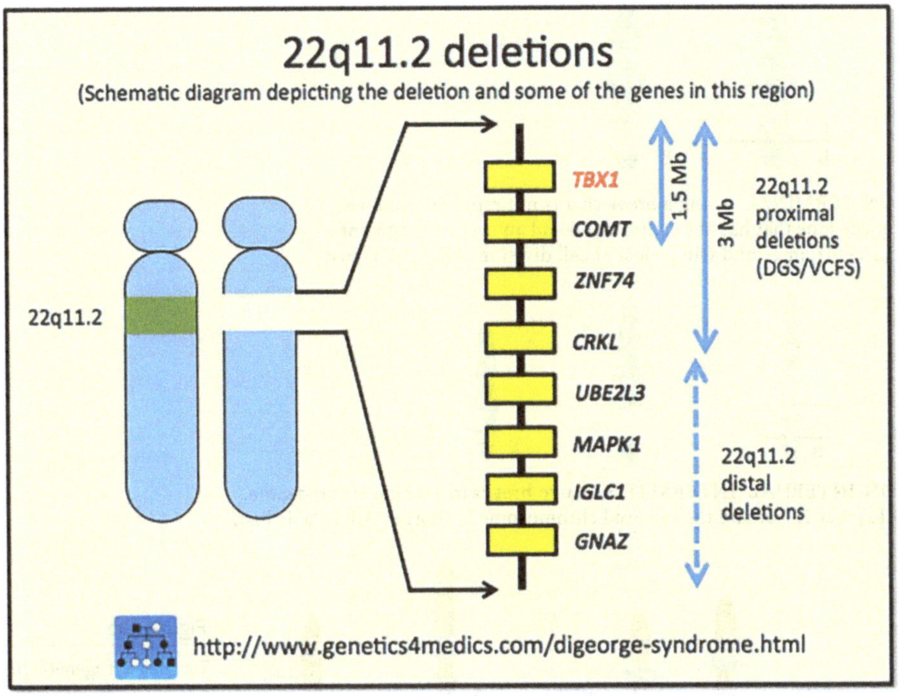

Figure 4.11

DiGeorge syndrome: Chromosome 22 deletion

Dr. Barr shows us other types of structural abnormalities in human chromosomes that have been observed to cause genetic disorders: These include, **duplications, inversions,** and **translocations.**

How does this happen, we wonder? Structural chromosome rearrangements generally result from chromosome breakage, either caused by environmental agents such as radiation and toxic chemicals. They can also result from cellular processes that make mistakes.

For example, genetic recombination is supposed to occur between homologous chromosomes. Sometimes nonhomologous chromosomes accidentally recombine causing a **reciprocal translocation.** Small deletions and duplications can result from mistakes in copying the DNA during replication where there the enzyme leaves out or inserts extra base pairs. There are repair enzymes that can correct these errors, but they don't always catch every mistake.

Fluorescent *in Situ* Hybridization (FISH)

We're interested to learn more about how genes can be identified at specific chromosomal locations. We are invited to the lab of Dr. Stefan Hell. We are very surprised when he asks us if we want to go fishing! Well, we reply politely, maybe another time, but right now we want to learn more about how to find genes on chromosomes. Dr. Hell laughs—that's exactly what we are going to do—fish

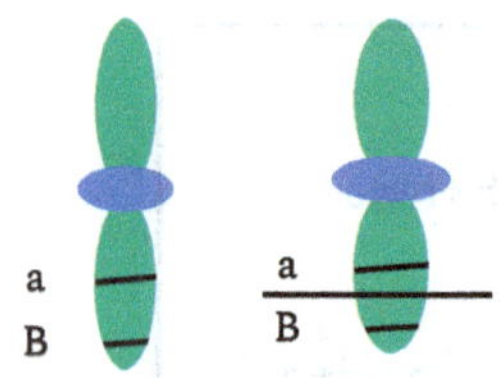

1. DELETION-TERMINAL: a single break that is not repaired produces a centric piece (one that has the centromere) and an acentric segment that lacks a centromere and will be lost at cell division. Allele 'B' is lost.

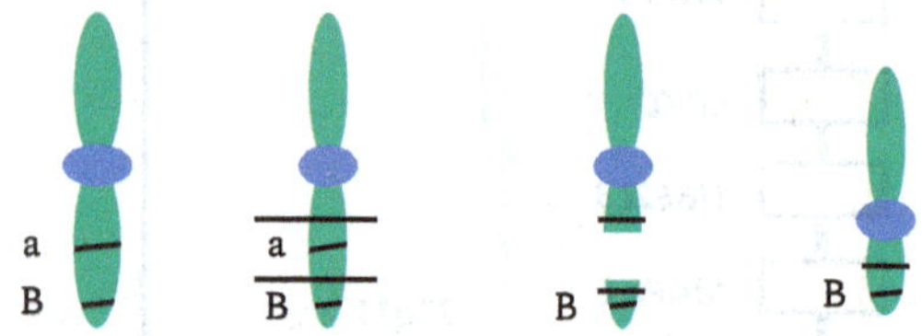

2. DELETION-INTERNAL (INTERSTITIAL): two breaks in a single chromosome. The middle piece is lost and the repaired chromosome is shorter. Allele 'a' is lost.

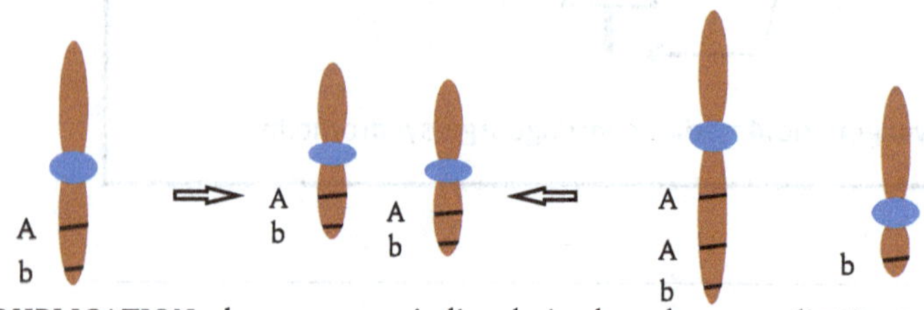

3. DUPLICATION: chromosomes misalign during homologous replication. One product has a duplicate copy of allele 'A'; the other has none.

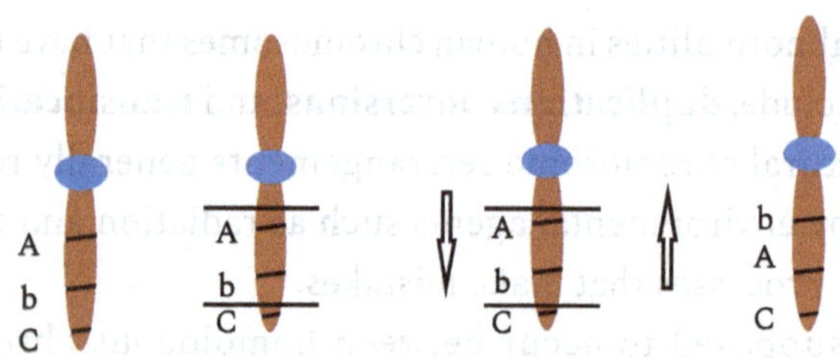

4. INVERSION: two breaks in a single chromosome; piece flips around and repaired in opposite direction. Order of alleles 'A b C' is now 'b A C'.

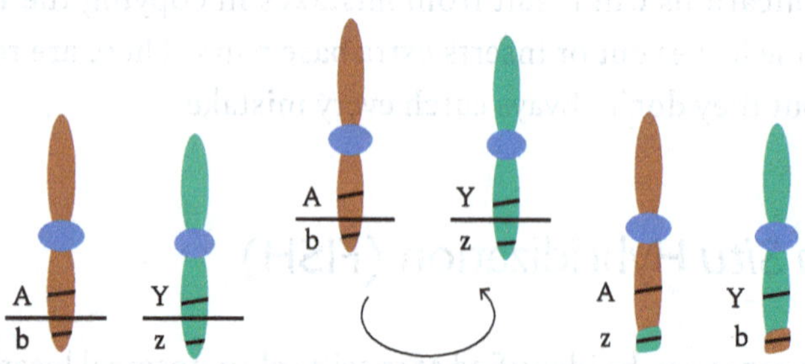

5. RECIPROCAL TRANSLOCATION: chromosomes with different genes (non-homologous) exchange segments by recombination. Alleles b and z are now on the wrong chromosomes.

Figure 4.12

Tutorial: Cytogenetic rearrangements

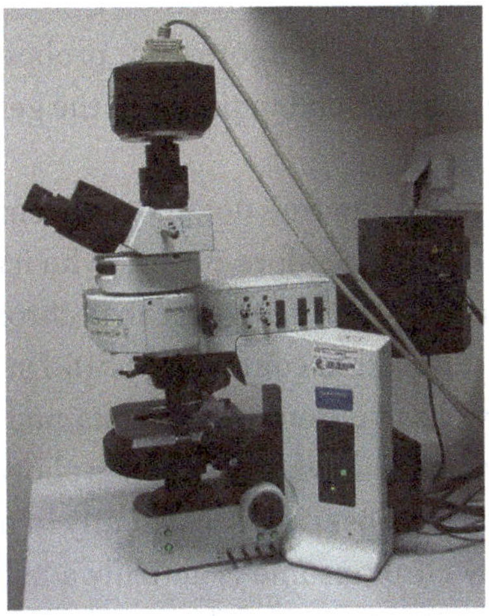

Figure 4.13

Fluorescence microscope

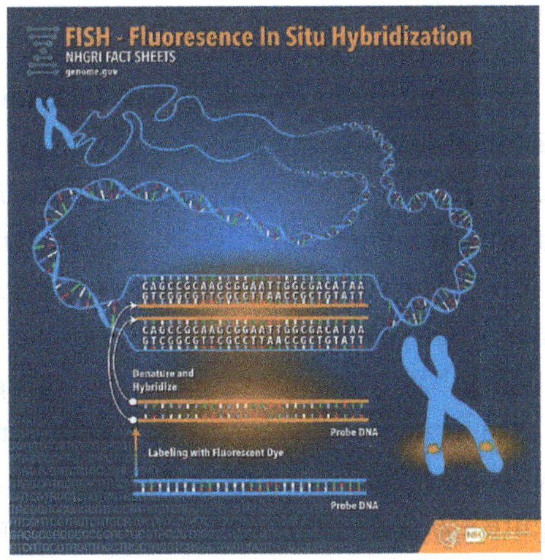

Figure 4.14

FISH technique

for genes on chromosomes! We begin to wonder if we've come to the right place, but we decide we'll give "fishing" for genes a try and go inside a large laboratory where he shows us a fluorescence microscope (see Figures 4.13 and 4.14).

"I helped invent this microscope," he tells us. "It can be used to determine the specific locations of genes on chromosomes that are targeted by a fluorescent probe specific to a single gene." This sounds like a very powerful imaging tool. We decide to take a closer look. We look inside the microscope focused on a DNA sample. The DNA absorbs the blue light and transmits a green fluorescent glow. We look more closely at the image (see Figure 4.15).

What we see under the lens what looks like a small universe. We are told that the two green spots are lighted probes that recognize chromosome 13 and the two red spots identify the two copies of chromosome 22.

Next, we are shown chromosomes from a child with DiGeorge syndrome, which results from a deletion on one copy of chromosome 22. The red label identifies the region on chromosome 22 that is deleted in patients with this genetic disorder. There is only one chromosome labeled, indicating that the corresponding site on the second copy of chromosome 22 is

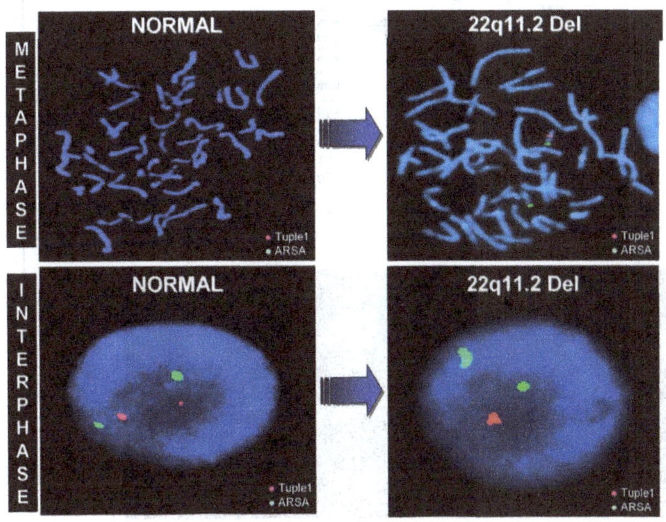

Figure 4.15

FISH analysis of DiGeorge syndrome

missing. We are very impressed. FISHing for specific genes using fluorescent probes as "lures" is a powerful way to identify the chromosomal locations of genes and to pinpoint the genetic origins of cytogenetic disorders.

The tools and techniques of cytogenetics allow us to see the fine details of chromosomes and genes. We have been invited to revisit the laboratory of Dr. Theodore Boveri, who has developed a very interesting theory of chromosomes and cancer. His studies suggest that chromosome abnormalities may contribute to the cause of cancer. Dr. Boveri is conferring with Dr. Nowell this afternoon, who has brought some interesting photographs of chromosomes obtained from his patients with a rare form of leukemia called chronic myeloid leukemia (CML). He shows Dr. Boveri the unusually small chromosome—number 22—that he has observed consistently in patients with CML (see Figure 4.2). Dr. Boveri explains that this tiny chromosome is actually a hybrid of chromosomes 22 and 9 that have exchanged pieces as a consequence of an abnormal event called a **reciprocal translocation.**

We look under the microscope and view chromosomes 9 and 22 rearrangements due to the reciprocal translocation (see Figure 4.16). **FISH analysis** has shown that a gene called "c-abl" has been transferred from its normal location on chromosome 9 to chromosome 22 where it is not regulated properly and leads to the abnormal growth and proliferation of the cell in which the translocation occurred and all its descendants (see Figure 4.17).

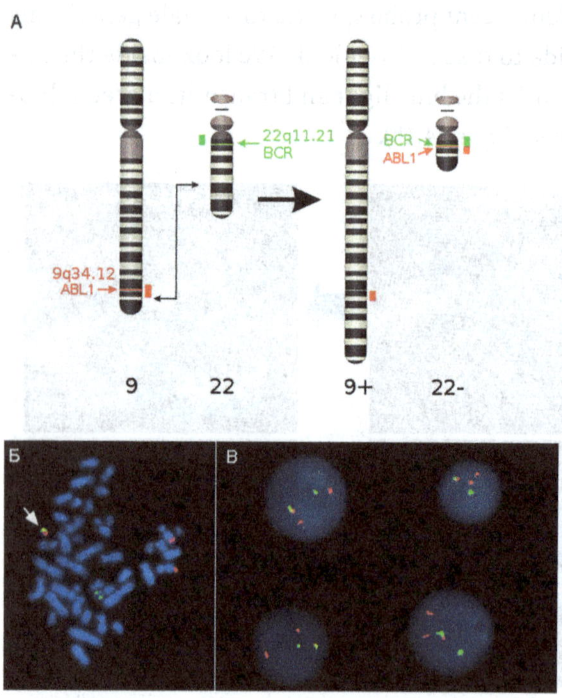

Figure 4.16

FISH and karyotype analysis of the Philadelphia chromosome

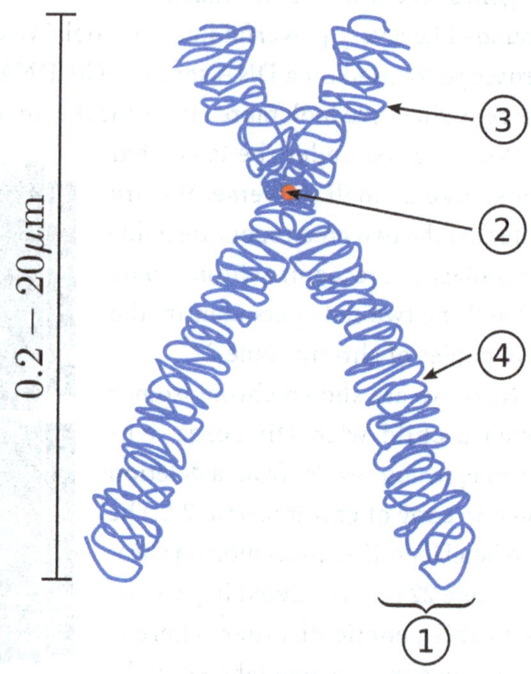

Figure 4.17

Chromosome diagram

"This is truly remarkable!" exclaims Dr. Boveri as he shakes hands with Dr. Nowell. "You have shown my theory to be correct. For the first time, a specific chromosome abnormality has been identified as a cause of cancer—leukemia!" We feel very fortunate to witness this amazing revelation. Now that the abnormal gene has been discovered, gene targeted drugs can fight the cancer by blocking the effects of this translocation on the growth of leukemia cells.

Use Figure 4.17 to answer the questions that follow.

4. **Identify the short arm: A. 1, B. 2, C. 3, or D. 4**
5. **Identify the long arm of the chromosome: A. 1, B. 2, C. 3, or D. 4**
6. **Identify the centromere: A. 1, B. 2, C. 3, or D. 4**
7. **Identify the sister chromatid: A. 1, B. 2, C. 3, or D. 4**

We want to learn more about genes what they look like and how they control all the processes that occur inside the cell. "For that," explains Dr. Boveri, "you will have to look at the DNA—the nucleic acid—of which genes are made. You must pay a visit to Dr. Watson."

So, off we go to the lab of Dr. James Watson to learn more about this chemical called DNA.

Reference

Nowell, Peter C., "Discovery of the Philadelphia Chromosome: A Personal Perspective," *Journal of Clinical Investigation* 117, no. 8 (2007): 2033–2035.

Figure Credits

Fig. 4.15: Copyright © Adriano R Tonelli1, Kalyan Kosuri1, Sainan Wei2, and Davoren Chick (CC BY 2.0) at https://commons.wikimedia.org/wiki/File:Fish_analysis_di_george_syndrome.jpg.

Fig. 4.16: Copyright © Philadelphia Chromosom.svg-Master Uegly (CC BY 3.0) at https://commons.wikimedia.org/wiki/File:Philadelphia_chromosome_detection.jpg.

Fig. 4.17: Copyright © Tryphon (CC BY 3.0) at https://commons.wikimedia.org/wiki/File:Chromosome.svg.

Chapter 5

DNA: The Genetic Material

Important Discoveries

The discovery in 1953 of the double helix, the twisted-ladder structure of deoxyribonucleic acid (DNA), by James Watson and Francis Crick marked a milestone in the history of science and gave rise to modern molecular biology, which is largely concerned with understanding how genes control the chemical processes within. ... (The Francis Crick Papers, The Discovery of the Double Helix, 1951–1953*) National Library of Medicine.*

Figure 5.1

The Eagle Pub in winter

We arrive at the Cavendish Laboratory at Cambridge University on a cold February morning. We are looking for Dr. Watson. So, apparently, is everyone else. "Where has that man gone?" we hear a voice asking in the background. "As usual—he's at the Eagle!" is the response (see Figure 5.1).

We rush over to the Eagle Pub to find there's quite a commotion. There is a man sitting at a table—apparently playing with some kind of tinker toy—claiming he has found the secret of life! As things begin to get 'curious-er and curious-er,' another, slightly older man rushes in shouting, "No—don't take him away! That's Dr. Watson! He and I—well, sorry for the lack of introduction—by the way, my name is Francis Crick and I'm quite pleased to meet you all—we have discovered the secret of life—and there it is—the structure of DNA!"—he proclaims—pointing to the tinker toy staircase spiral structure on the table. The pub becomes very quiet as everyone stops to stare in amazement. The structure of DNA! We move in closer to listen as Dr. Watson explains what they have discovered:

> *I couldn't help, you know, just switching around on the table to see that adenine and thymine had a, formed a very nice base pair and guanine and cytosine formed one identical in shape, and I thought you can build a double helix with adenine and thymine and guanine and cytosine base pairs. (Watson,* The Double Helix*)*

This is truly remarkable—so much information hidden in the structure of a molecule. How did scientists discover that DNA was the genetic material? To learn more about this, we leave the pub and go back to the laboratory where we find Dr. Frederick Griffith busy at work studying how genetic properties are transmitted between bacterial cells. He invites us in to take a look at his most recent experiment. He is studying bacteria that can cause pneumonia in mice—called a pneumococcus. He has found that the bacteria can only cause infection if the cell is surrounded by a capsule. There are two strains of the pneumococcus—one that produces a capsule and can cause pneumonia and another strain that cannot form a capsule and cannot cause disease. He has discovered—amazingly—that if he takes dead bacteria that form capsules and mixes them with live bacteria that cannot make capsules—these live bacteria are somehow "transformed" by the dead cells into bacteria that now can make capsules and cause pneumonia! How can this happen? Dr. Griffith shows us what is going on (see Figure 5.2).

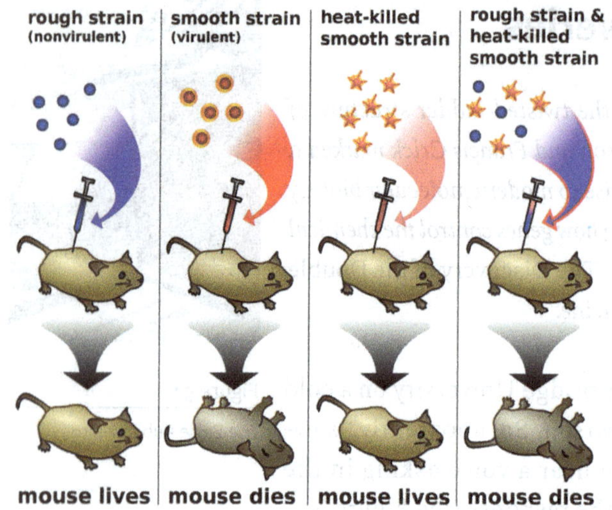

Figure 5.2

Griffith's experiment

Figure 5.3

Frederich Miescher's laboratory in Tubingen

1. **What was it in the dead bacterial cells that allowed the live bacteria to acquire the ability to make capsules?**

So—the genetic material goes from the dead cells to the live cells—transforming them into cells that can make a capsule! And this is DNA. What kind of a molecule can do this?

Dr. Griffith tells us that many years ago Dr. Friedrich Miescher determined the chemical makeup of what he called "nuclein." We go to visit Dr. Miescher's lab where he is purifying the components of DNA (see Figure 5.3).

Dr. Miescher has identified several compounds from the nucleus: phosphate, deoxyribose sugar, and several nitrogenous bases: adenine, guanine, thymine, and cytosine. "It was very easy," he says, "DNA contains very few molecules: sugar, phosphate, and a couple of bases." "Is that all?" we ask. "Yes," he says, "let's take a closer look" (see Figure 5.4).

The nitrogen-containing bases are linked to sugar and phosphate to form **nucleotides**: the building blocks of DNA. For example, this is the nucleotide of adenine: the base is linked to a 5-carbon sugar—called **deoxyribose**—and the sugar is linked to a phosphate group.

2. **Which carbon on the deoxyribose sugar attaches to the nitrogenous base?**
3. **Which carbon on the deoxyribose sugar is attached to the 5' phosphate in a nucleotide?**

So that's it—four nucleotides! "How can the chemical composition of the genetic material be so simple?" we ask. "Do you think maybe you made a mistake?" Dr. Miescher glares at us, indignant.

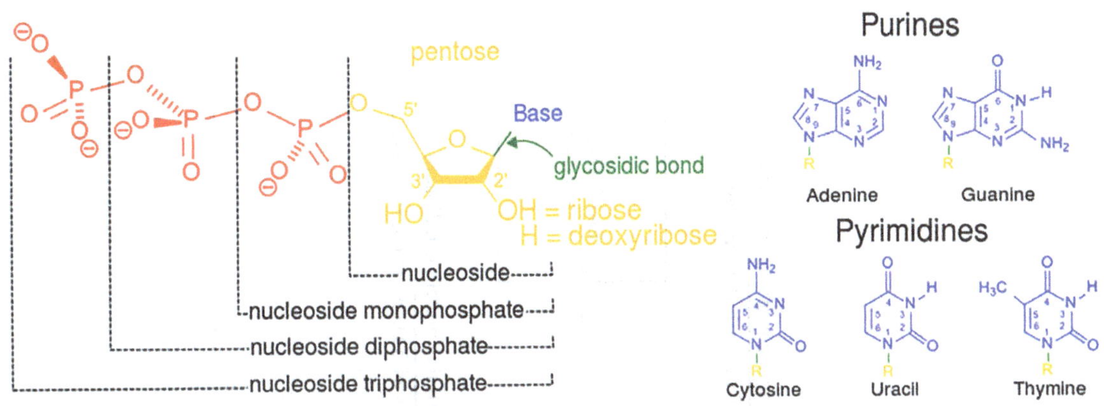

Figure 5.4

The building blocks of DNA

"Who said anything about the genetic material? This is what DNA is made of. I didn't say anything about the genetic material. That is ridiculous!"

It seems a lot of scientists agree with him. There's not a lot of support for the idea that DNA is the genetic material—it's just too simple! It would take a complex molecule to code for life—maybe a protein?

Dr. Miescher is anxious to return to his chemistry so he sends us to visit Dr. Oswald Avery who is attempting to determine whether DNA or protein is the genetic material. "We think it's got to be protein—but all our experiments say it's DNA. We don't know what to think." He seems discouraged. He perks up when he gets a call from Drs. Alfred Hershey and Martha Chase. They're over at the Cold Spring Harbor Laboratory studying the genetic material of viruses. He suggests we all go over and pay them a visit. "Isn't that where they study eugenics?" we ask, feeling a little uncomfortable. "Not anymore," Dr. Avery reassures us, "they're doing real science now!"

We hurry to the harbor where there seems to be a lot of excitement over Hershey and Chase's latest findings. We take a closer look to find out what's going on (see Figure 5.5).

Dr. Chase explains what's happening. They did two experiments using radioactive tracers (shown in red) to label either the DNA or the protein of the virus. In the first experiment shown in the top part of the figure, DNA is labeled. You can see that when the radioactive phage get inside the bacterial cell it is the radioactive DNA that is controlling the genetics of the phage because the inside of the bacterial cell is radioactive—she pulls out the Geiger counter and we hear it blasting!

In the second experiment, they labeled the protein part of the phage with a radioactive tracer, not the DNA. This time the radioactivity stayed outside the cell and the part of the phage (the genes) that gets inside the bacterial cell is not radioactive. We stop to listen, but we hear no noise! Therefore, it is the DNA that gets inside the bacteria to control the formation of new phage genes and protein—the genetic material is DNA!

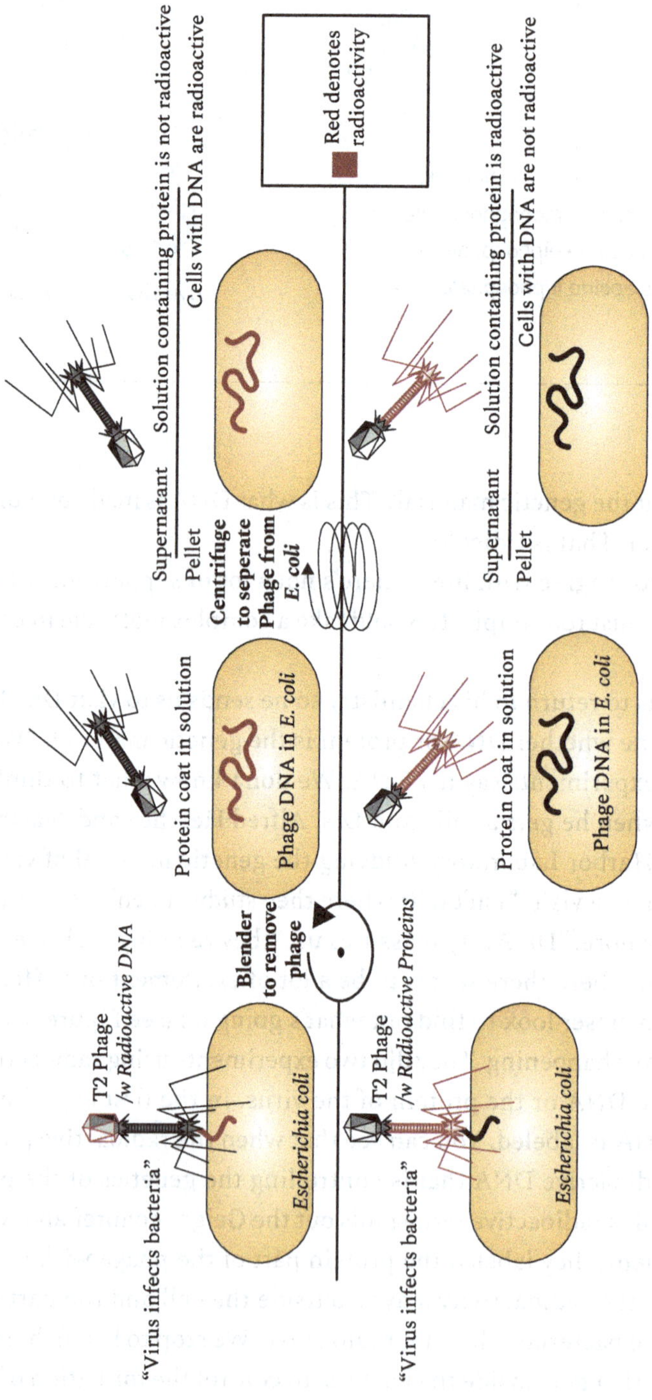

Figure 5-5

Hershey Chase experiment

What an elegant experiment! Using these highly specific radioactive tracers, there can be no doubt that DNA carries the genetic information.

4. **Why does the fact that the bacterial cells take up the radioactive phosphorus show that DNA is the genetic material?**

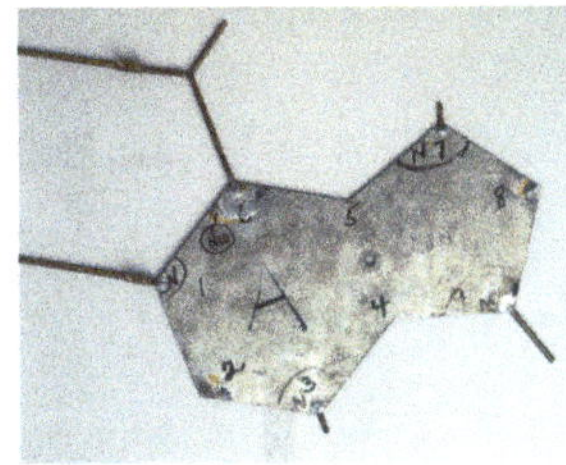

Figure 5.6

Original piece from Crick and Watson's DNA molecular model, 1953

The Double Helix

But how does all this work? How can such a simple molecule be "the secret of life"! To answer that question, we return to the Cavendish Laboratory where Drs. Watson and Crick have now returned after their morning of celebration at the Eagle Pub and are busy writing a research paper on their findings on the structure of DNA. "What do you think?" we ask. "How can such a simple molecule be the blueprint of life?" Watson and Crick give each other a knowing glance. "Well, let us SHOW you—it's all in the structure! The structure of DNA is the secret of life." We decide to take a closer look at the metal cutouts Watson has placed in front of us (see Figures 5.6 and 5.7).

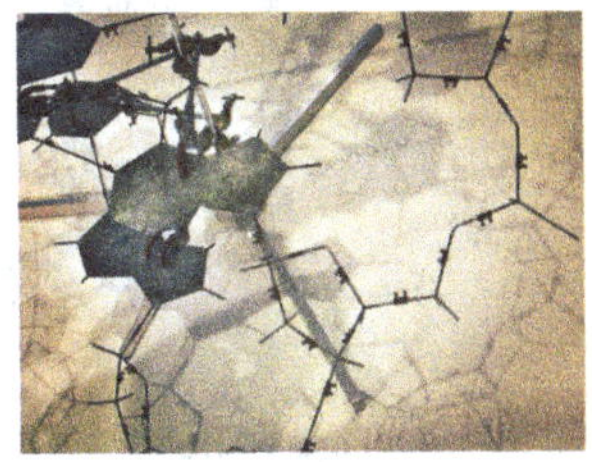

Figure 5.7

The famous Watson-Crick model of the double helix

We take a look at the finely cut metal pieces in the model that swirl and spire seemingly upward into the sky. "How did you determine that this was the molecular structure of DNA?" we ask.

We notice some test tubes with clumps of white material on the bottom. Dr. Watson explains that these are fibers of DNA that have been extracted from cells. "You figured out the structure of DNA by looking at this?!" we ask incredulously (see Figure 5.8). "Oh, no! We got a little help from our friends. ..."

Figure 5.8

Freshly prepared test tubes of DNA fibers extracted from cells

Dr. Watson pulls out a glossy photo from his desk (see Figure 5.9).

This is an image showing the X-ray diffraction pattern produced by crystals of DNA fibers. Dr. Rosalind Franklin prepared these fibers and carried out these studies (see Figure 5.10). What you see looks like an X-ray showing spots, but the spots are actually generated as a unique pattern that reveals the structure of the molecule that produced this pattern. Detailed analysis of the DNA X-ray diffraction pattern tells a lot about the structure of DNA, its simple repetitive molecular structure revealed by the position of the bands and spots on the image.

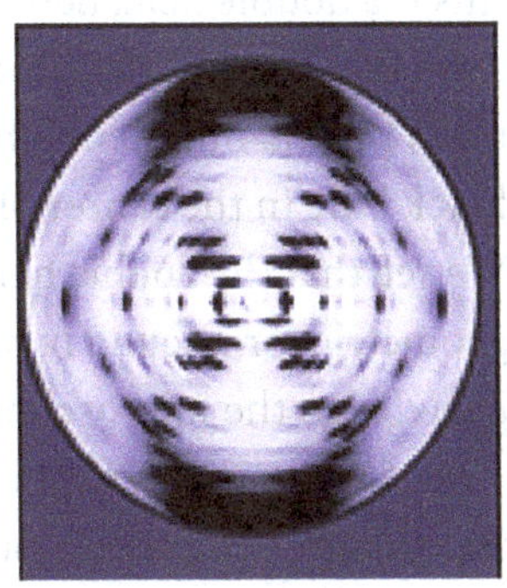

Figure 5.9

DNA X-ray diffraction pattern

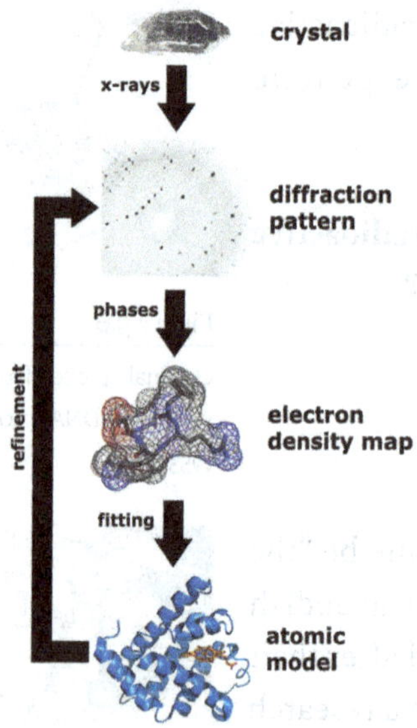

Figure 5.10

Steps in preparing DNA crystals for X-ray diffraction studies

This is the photograph that revealed the mystery of DNA: its structure precisely defines its function. It transforms this incredibly simple batch of chemicals into a universal code of life. This is what the photo revealed (see Figure 5.11).

So—there it is—the double helix—so simple—so elegant (see Figure 5.12).

"Is this DNA?" we ask. We are told that this is a double helix nebula. The spots are stars lit up by infrared imaging. This nebula is several hundred light years from the black hole in the center of the Milky Way. We see that the double helix is a repeating geometric form found in nature from large galaxies to the microscopic core of life.

Dr. Watson interrupts abruptly. He is anxious to get back to our conversation about the DNA double helix (the one he's

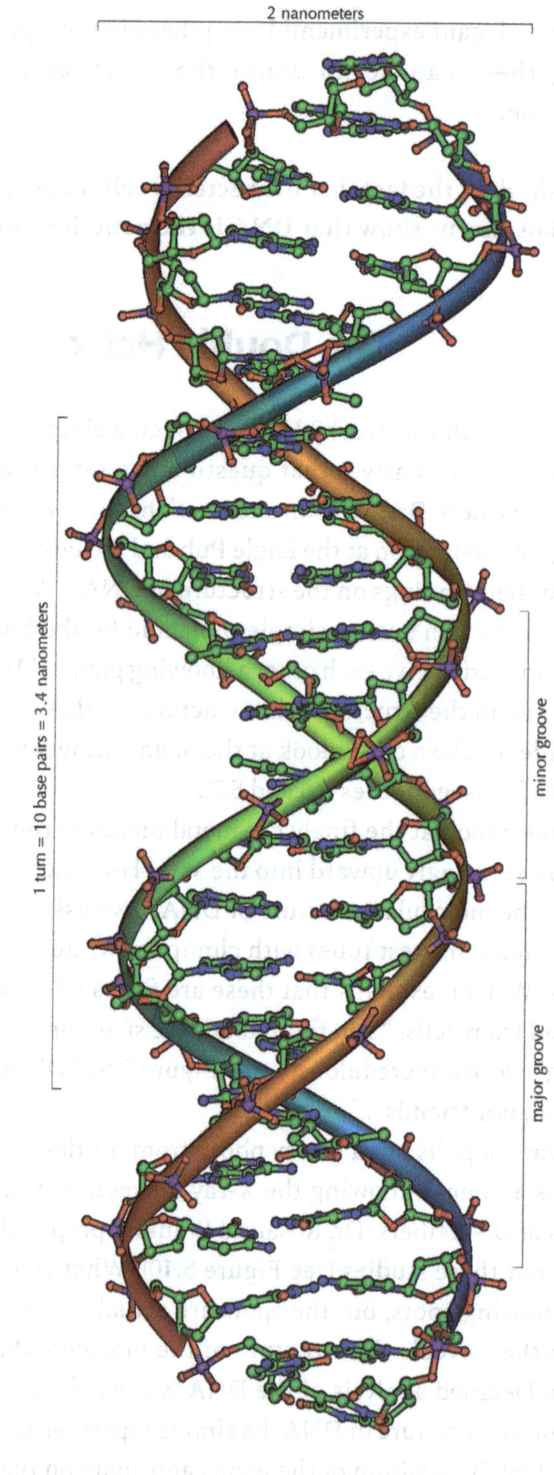

Figure 5.11

DNA structure revealed by X-ray diffraction pattern

Figure 5.12

The double helix nebula

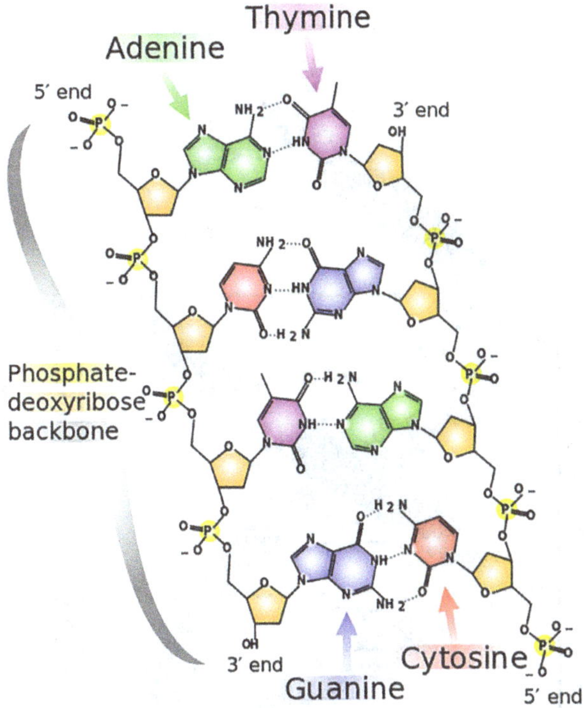

Figure 5.13

The biochemical structure of DNA

famous for discovering)! We listen carefully as Dr. Watson describes the structure of the DNA helix in more detail:

> *Dr. Watson explains, "We had to make the strands run in opposite directions in our model to make it consistent with the X-ray image of its structure—otherwise—if the strands were running in the same direction the helix would have an uneven diameter. (Watson,* The Double Helix*)*

DNA Structure

The steps of the staircase consist of the nitrogen-containing bases that are attached to the backbone by covalent linkage to the sugar (see Figure 5.13). Each step consists of a pair of bases. We immediately notice that the paired bases on each step are either **adenine-thymine** or **cytosine-guanine.** We don't see any adenine-guanine, adenine-cytosine, guanine-thymine or cytosine-thymine base pairs. "We learned that from Dr. Chargaff," Watson says. "His research on the DNA content of different species showed that the amount of adenine always equals the amount of thymine and

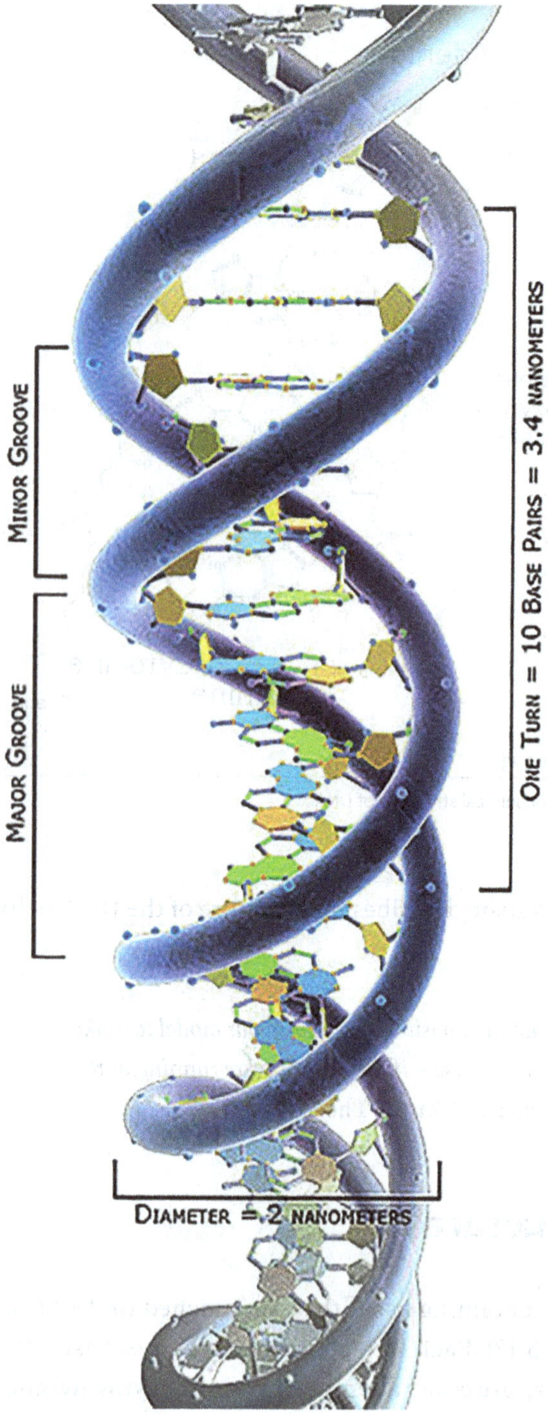

Figure 5.14

The spatial dimensions of the double helix

the amount of guanine always is the same as the amount of cytosine in all types of DNA. He calls this the *base-pairing rules.*"

The base pairs are held together loosely by hydrogen bonds, so they can come apart. "Precisely!" exclaims Dr. Watson. "This is how Dr. Crick and I figured out how the DNA makes copies of itself. The base pairs come apart, and because of Dr. Erwin Chargaff's **base-pairing rules**, we know that each strand can form a new strand that is the complement of itself simply by following the base-pairing rules." This is incredible—the DNA is a self-replicating molecule! We want to learn more about how this works.

Please refer to Figure 5.14 to answer the following questions:

5. **What is the diameter of the double helix?**
6. **How many nanometers per turn of the helix?**
7. **How many base pairs per turn of the helix?**

DNA Replication

Well, the model for DNA replication certainly makes a lot of sense! "But how did you prove that this is actually the way DNA replication happens?" we ask. Dr. Watson sends us back to Cold Spring Harbor Laboratory where Drs. Matthew Meselson and Franklin Stahl are attempting a very elegant experiment to determine how the process of replication works (see Figure 5.15).

8. **How is the isotope N15 labeled DNA distinguished from the nonlabeled N14 DNA?**

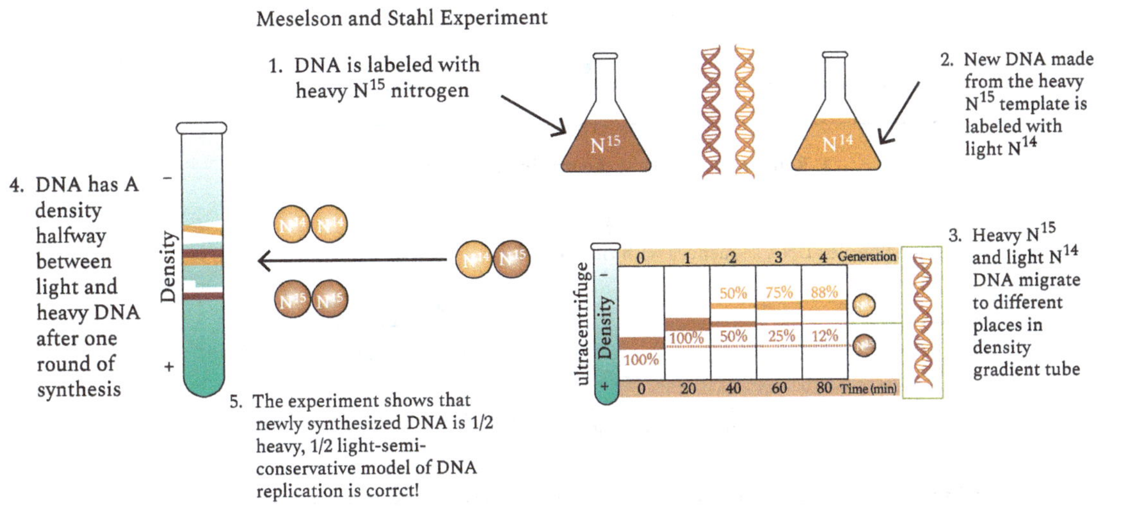

Figure 5.15

Tutorial: The Meselson and Stahl experiment

9. **Why is all the DNA synthesized in one generation all heavy/light hybrid?**
10. **What would the DNA look like after one generation if replication was conservative rather than semi-conservative?**

We are thinking about this incredibly elegant process—replication and how it happens. We take a closer look at each step of replication and the enzymes involved (see Figure 5.16).

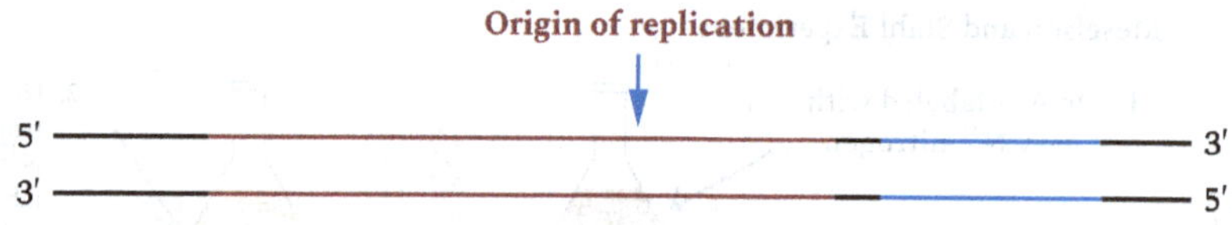

1. Replicatin begins at the origin of replication

Unzipping duplex DNA sequences with rich AT

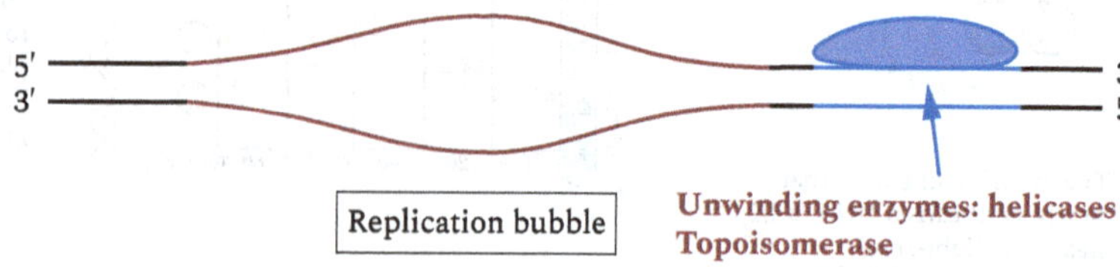

In bacteria, that have only a small circular DNA, there is only one **origin of replication (OR)** called *Ori C*- in eukaryotes, there are multiple origins at no specific location along the length of the chromosome.

2. The DNA strands separate.
   - Enzymes called **topoisomerases** and **gyrases** uncoil the helix.
   - **Helicases** break the hydrogen bonds holding the two strands of the helix together.
   - **Single stranded DNA binding proteins (ssbs)** hold the DNA strands apart so they don't reform the helix.

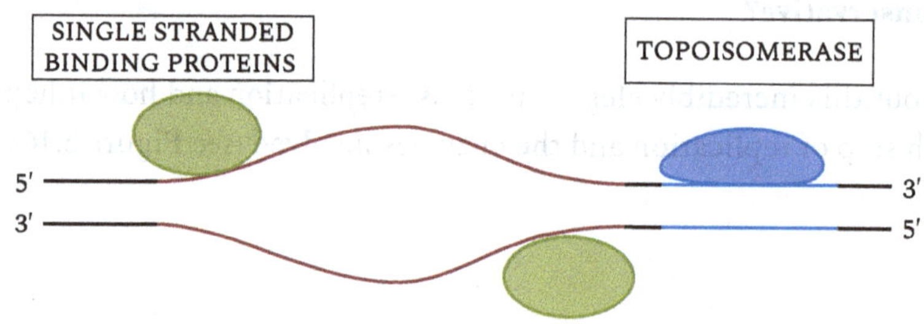

3. Replication proceeds in both directions away from the origin, creating a **left fork** and a **right fork**.
   - The forks are located at the junction of single-stranded and double-stranded DNA.

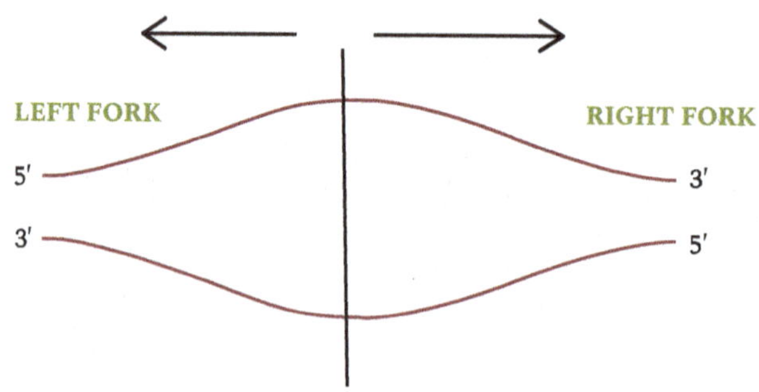

4. A **primase** places a short string of RNA nucleotides to serve as a **primer** for replication since DNA polymerase cannot begin a new strand.

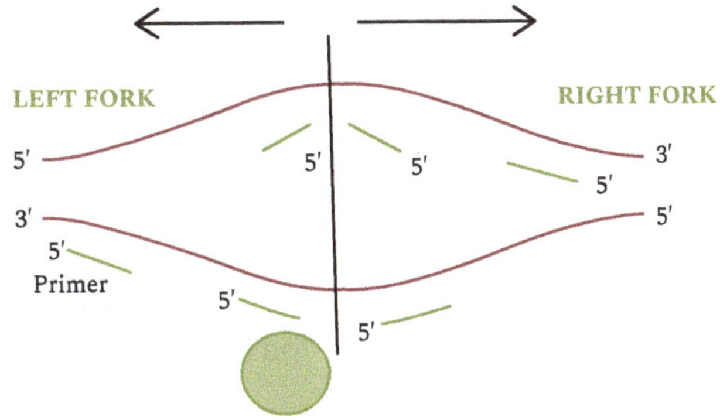

5. **DNA polymerase** (**DNA Pol III**) adds nucleotides to the **3'OH** of each chain, only moving in the 5' to 3' direction to form leading and lagging strands.

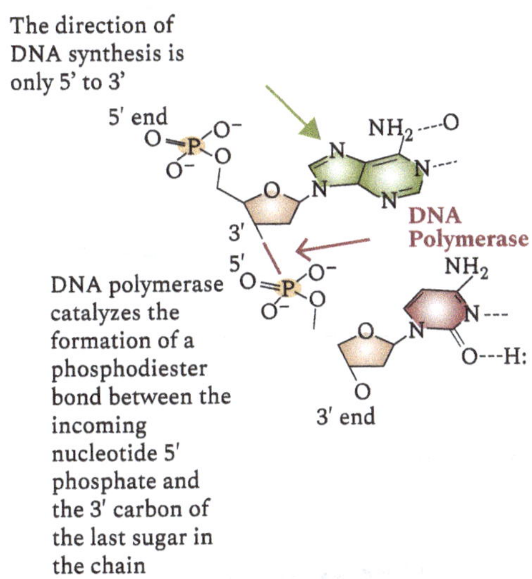

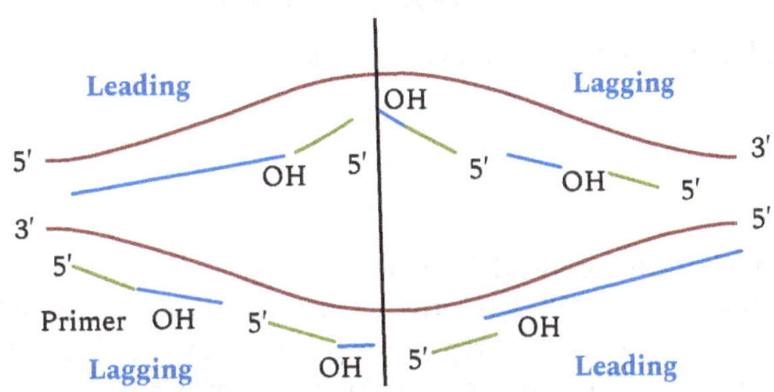

- The **leading strand** is synthesized in the same direction as the fork, moving away from the origin-this is called the **continuous strand** since it is made all in one piece using a single primer.
- The **lagging strand** is synthesized **5′ to 3′** in the opposite direction away from the fork towards the origin -and this is accomplished by making individual short pieces each with its own primer called **Okazaki fragments** 5′ ——— 3′. This is called **discontinuous synthesis**.

6. Another **DNA polymerase** (**Pol I**) cuts out the RNA primers and fills in the spaces with DNA nucleotides.

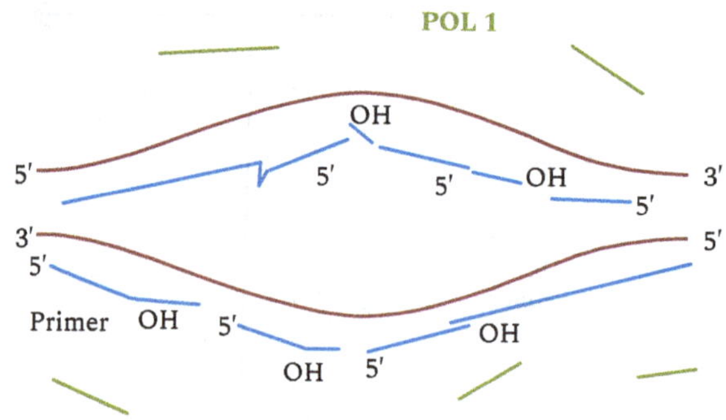

7. An enzyme called **ligase** seals up the gaps between 5' phosphate and 3'OH groups to make a complete DNA strands that spontaneously fold to form a new helix.

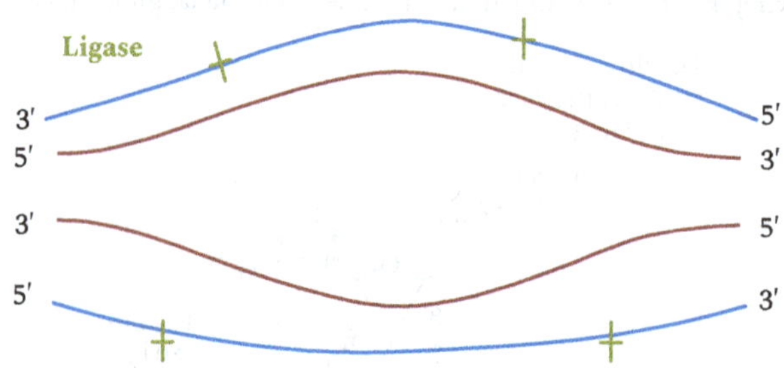

Figure 5.16

Tutorial: DNA replication

Next we learn all about the genetic code.

Reference

Watson, James. *The Double Helix*. Simon and Shuster, 1968.

Figure Credits

Fig. 5.1: Source: https://en.wikipedia.org/wiki/File:Eaglepub.jpg

Fig. 5.2: Copyright © Madprime (CC BY 3.0) at https://commons.wikimedia.org/wiki/File:Griffith_experiment.svg.

Fig. 5.3: "Fredreich Miescher's Laboratory," http://www.genome.gov/25520232. 1879.

Fig. 5.4: Source: https://commons.wikimedia.org/wiki/File:Nucleotides_1.svg

Fig. 5.5: Copyright © Adenosine (CC BY 2.5) at https://commons.wikimedia.org/wiki/File:HersheyChaseEx.png.

Fig. 5.6: Copyright © Science Museum London/Science and Society Picture Library (CC BY 2.0) at https://commons.wikimedia.org/wiki/File:Template_from_Crick_and_Watson%E2%80%99s_DNA_molecular_model,_1953._(9660573227).jpg.

Fig. 5.7: Copyright © Stew Dean (CC BY 2.0) at https://www.flickr.com/photos/58109753@N00/18717400.

Fig. 5.8: Source: https://commons.wikimedia.org/wiki/File:DNA01525_50.JPG

Fig. 5.9: Source: https://en.wikibooks.org/wiki/File:Xray_DNA.gif

Fig. 5.10: Copyright © Thomas Splettstoesser (CC BY-SA 3.0) at https://commons.wikimedia.org/wiki/File:X_ray_diffraction.png.
Fig. 5.11: Copyright © Michael Ströck (CC BY-SA 3.0) at https://commons.wikimedia.org/wiki/File:DNA_Overview.png.
Fig. 5.12: Source: https://commons.wikimedia.org/wiki/File:False-Color_Image_of_Double_Helix_Nebula.jpg
Fig. 5.13: Source: https://commons.wikimedia.org/wiki/File:DNA_chemical_structure.svg
Fig. 5.14: Copyright © Zygote Media Group (CC BY 2.5) at https://commons.wikimedia.org/wiki/File:3DScience_DNA_structure_labeled_a.jpg.
Fig.5.15: Source: https://commons.wikimedia.org/wiki/File:Meselson-stahl_experiment_diagram_en.svg
Fig. 5.16: Adapted from Copyright © Emply Shell China dry (CC BY-SA 3.0) at https://commons.wikimedia.org/wiki/File:Figure_Role_of_initiators_for_initiation_of_DNA_replication.png.

Chapter 6

Unraveling the Code of Life

What Causes Cystic Fibrosis?

We receive word that there has been an exciting development in the study of cystic fibrosis. We remember our earlier visit with a child suffering from this devastating genetic disorder and are very anxious to discover the exciting news! We arrive back at the laboratory of Dr. Dorothy Andersen where she is excitedly calling together an impromptu meeting with her research group (see Figure 6.1). “I have just identified a genetic disorder that that I am calling ‘cystic fibrosis’!” she proclaims triumphantly. She pulls out a complicated-looking map of chromosome 7 (see Figure 6.2). She directs our attention to a specific region of the q arm where the gene responsible for cystic fibrosis has been located. This gene is called “CFTR“ and codes for a protein, the “cystic fibrosis transmembrane conductance channel,“ that regulates membrane conductance of chloride ions in the lungs and other organs of the body (see Figure 6.3). Dr. Andersen pulls out a map of this gene that shows its DNA sequence. She then shows us the DNA sequence of the CFTR gene from a young boy with cystic fibrosis. “It is missing three nucleotides,” she explains. “Is that all?” we ask. “What do you mean, ‘is that all’?” she says, apparently growing more agitated by the second. We attempt to justify ourselves by explaining that cystic fibrosis is such a devastating disorder that results in death if not treated. “How could a disorder with such a huge effect on the body result from removing only three bases from a gene that is at least a thousand bases in length?” “To find the answer to that question,” she advises, “you will have to visit Dr. Nirenberg.” “He has just cracked the genetic code!” That sounds very mysterious—the genetic code—how does it work? We hurry to visit Dr. Marshall Warren Nirenberg to learn more.

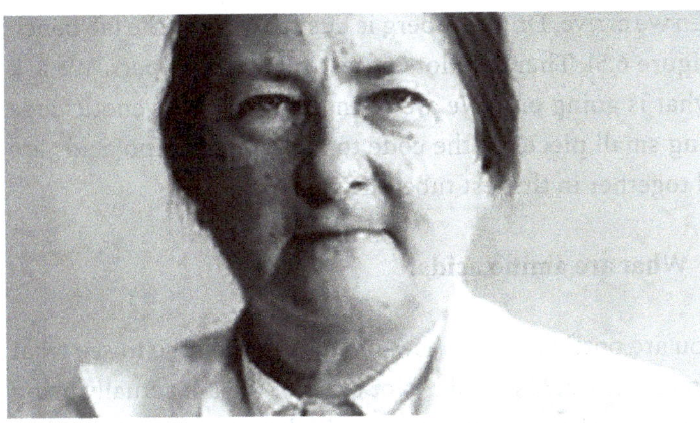

Figure 6.1

Dr. Dorothy Andersen

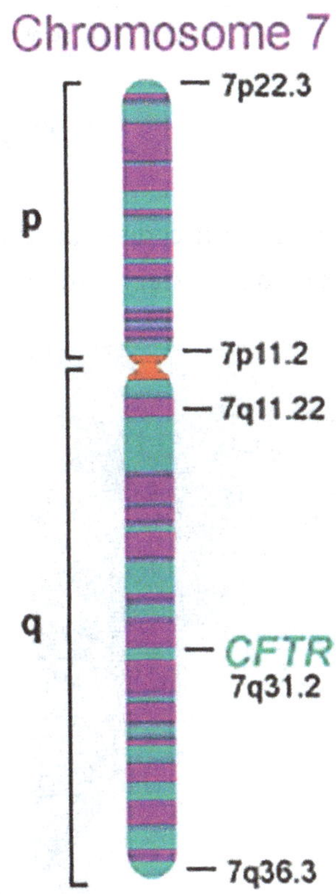

Figure 6.2

Chromosome 7 cystic fibrosis gene

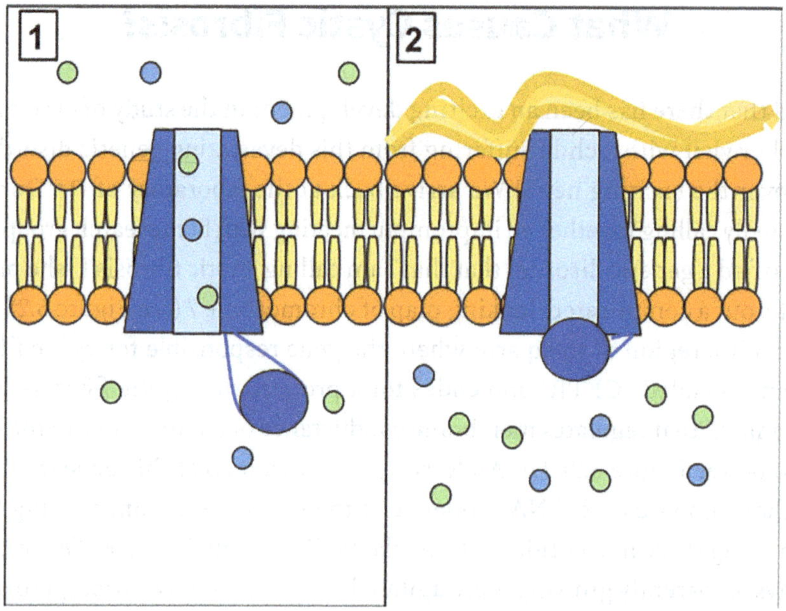

Figure 6.3

Defect in CFTR membrane channel

Cracking the Code of Life

DNA—the genetic code—like the Rosetta Stone it allows us to unravel a secret language—one that has remained a mystery until very modern times (see Figure 6.4).

Figure 6.4

The Rosetta Stone

How did it happen? How was the genetic code deciphered? We are on our way to visit the laboratory where the "secret of life," the molecular language of DNA, was first decoded.

When we arrive, Dr. Nirenberg is busy at work at the lab bench (see Figure 6.5). There are lots of test tubes and pipets. We ask him what is going on. "We are trying to crack the genetic code by using small pieces of the code to see which amino acids are linked together in the test tube," he explains.

1. **What are amino acids?**

"So, you are putting little pieces of DNA in the tube to see what protein comes out?" we ask. "Not exactly. We are actually using **messenger RNA** nucleotides to see which amino acids are linked together."

Figure 6.5

Dr. Nirenberg cracks the genetic code

'Messenger RNA? What is that?" we ask. "I can't help you," Dr. Nirenberg states flatly. "You need to talk to Dr. Crick."

Off we go! Dr. Crick is happy to explain that he predicted the existence of a messenger form of nucleic acid that would be copied from the DNA even before it was discovered. The gene must be copied to produce a molecule that carries the coding information to the cytoplasm where protein synthesis occurs in eukaryotes. Researchers found the molecule and named it **messenger RNA** (mRNA) (see Figure 6.6). Like DNA, this nucleic acid also contains four nucleotides; three are the same as in DNA-adenine, guanine and cytosine—but the pyrimidine thymine is replaced by the closely related pyrimidine uracil in RNA.

2. **Why is the coding information in DNA copied to messenger RNA?**

We take a closer look at the molecule—it looks similar to DNA, but we notice immediately that it is single stranded rather than double stranded. An even closer look reveals that the sugar is slightly

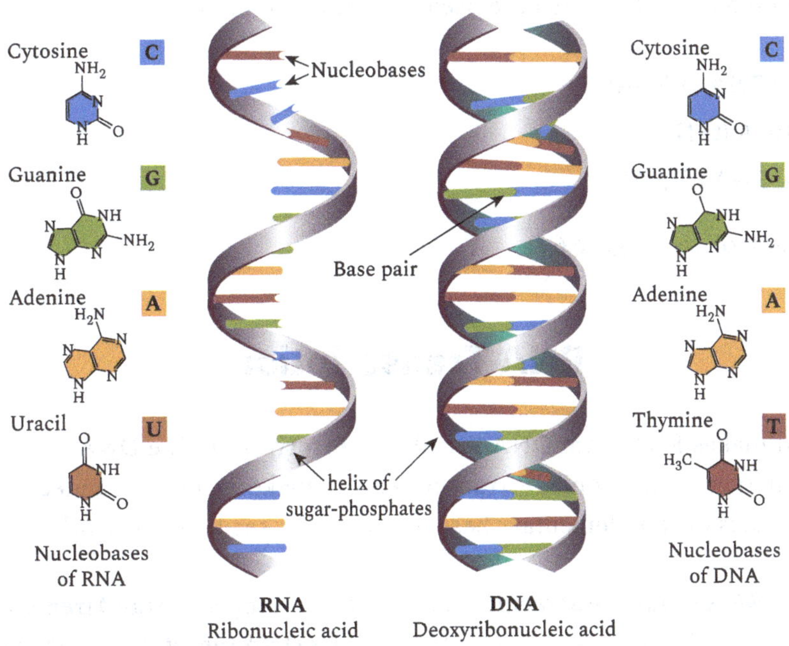

Figure 6.6

RNA versus DNA

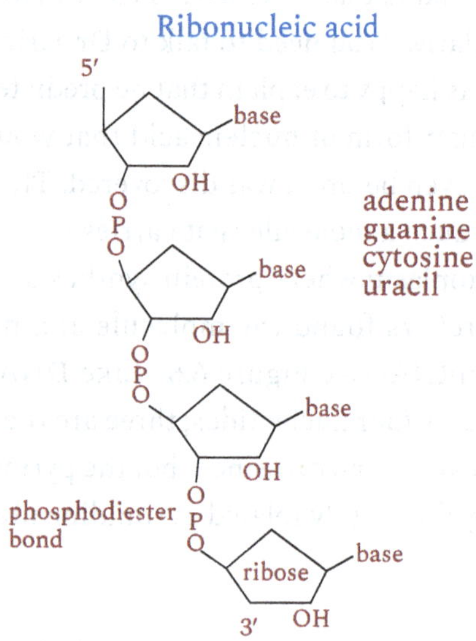

Figure 6.7

Three different types of RNA

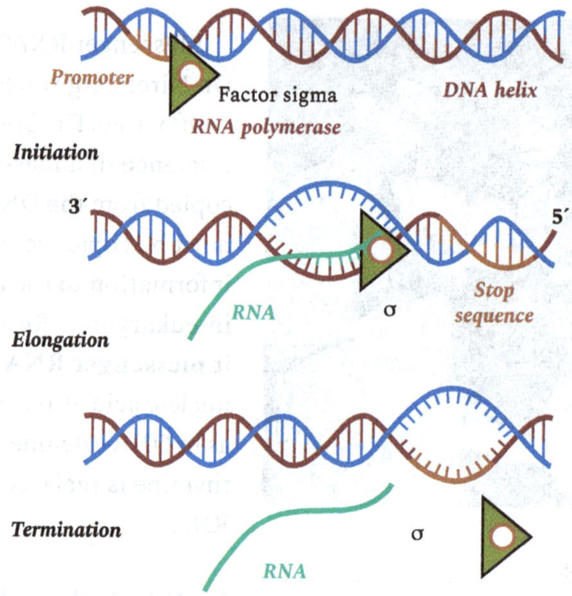

Figure 6.8

RNA transcription overview

different—it is a ribose sugar—hydrogen H is replaced by a hydroxide OH at the 2' position of the 5 carbon sugar.

There are several types of RNA that are used in gene expression:

- Messenger RNA (mRNA)
- Transfer RNA (tRNA)
- Ribosomal RNA (rRNA)

Let's take a closer look (see Figure 6.7).

RNA Transcription

The process that makes RNA from DNA is called **transcription.** The DNA bases that form the origins of the genetic code are copied—transcribed—to make a single-stranded copy of the gene just by using the rules of complementary base pairing. Let's see how this works (see Figure 6.8).

3. **Show the mRNA sequence determined by the DNA template strand (remember that RNA sequence is complementary and antiparallel to its DNA template) shown by the following transcript: 3'ccaggttacgtactatg 5'**

How does the cell find the gene it wants to copy to mRNA? It turns out that all genes contain signals that control which genes are copied and how often. These signals are called **promoters**. They are short pieces of DNA that are recognized by the enzymes and transcription factors that are used to make mRNA.

This is what a promoter looks like. Look at the gene shown in Figure 6.9.

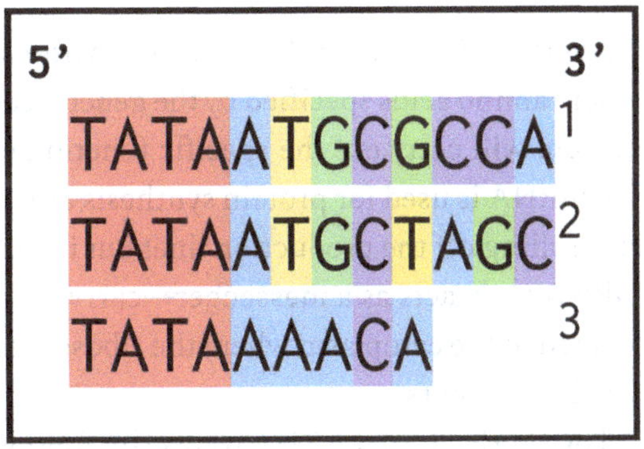

Figure 6.9

RNA promoter complex

We can see that the promoter is a short DNA sequence that is recognized by transcription factors that start the process of transcription. An important promoter called the "**TATA box**" has the core DNA sequence 5'-TATAAA-3' or a similar variant, which is usually followed by three or more adenine bases. It is usually located 25 to 35 base pairs upstream in the 5' direction of the transcription start site. The more ancient bacterial cells use a closely related promoter called the Pribnow box that contains the sequence TATAAT of six nucleotides (thymine—adenine—thymine—etc.) The AT-rich sequence of the TATA-box facilitates easy unwinding, due to weaker base-pairing interactions between A and T bases, as compared to between G and C.

The TATA box is usually found at the binding site of RNA polymerase II. TFIID, a transcription factor, initially binds to the TATA box, followed by transcription factors TFIIA and TFIIB. RNA polymerase can then recognize this multiprotein complex and bind to it to initiate the process of transcription. These transcription factors are called TATA-binding proteins (TBPs) and transcription factor IIB (TFIIBs) because they bind to the TATA box. Because TATA boxes are located adjacent to genes, when transcription factors bind to the TATA box, this opens up the double helix so the DNA can be copied to make messenger RNA. The DNA strand that is copied is called the **template strand.** RNA nucleotides base pair to the DNA bases of the template strand according to the base-pairing rules. This allows the production of a message that encodes the base sequence information of a specific gene. The sequence of bases in mRNA is held together by phosphodiester bonds linking covalently the sugar phosphate backbone catalyzed by the enzyme **RNA polymerase.** The RNA polymerase moves along the DNA template strand covalently linking the incoming nucleotides base-paired to the template DNA to form a single stranded mRNA.

4. **Find the TATA box and the transcription start site 25 bases downstream from this promoter:**
GAATTCTAATCTCCCTCTCAACCCTACAGTCACCCATTTGGTATATTAAAGAT GTGTTGTCTACTGTCTAGTATCCCTCAAGTAGTGTCAGGAATTAGTCATTTAA ATAGTCTGCAAGCCAGGAGTGGTGGCTCATGTCTGTAATTCCAG

Once the mRNA is synthesized, it separates from the DNA template and binds to the ribosome where amino acids specified by the genetic code are linked together to make a specific protein. This protein will carry out the specific function specified by the instructions of the gene. In bacteria, the mRNA is used for protein synthesis as soon as it is made—this can occur while the message is still rolling off the production line! But in eukaryotes, transcription occurs in the nucleus and the mRNA truly acts as a messenger—carrying the genetic code from the nucleus where the DNA is located to the cytoplasm where the ribosomes are located—the site where **translation**—or protein synthesis occurs.

The synthesis of the RNA transcript follows similar steps in bacteria and in eukaryotic cells (see Figure 6.10).

1. Transcription initiation factors bind to the promoter at the beginning—or 5' end—of a specific gene.
2. The double helix separates to expose the sequence of bases on the template strand.
3. RNA polymerase binds to the promoter.
4. RNA nucleotides complementary to the sequence of bases on the DNA template strand form hydrogen bonds.

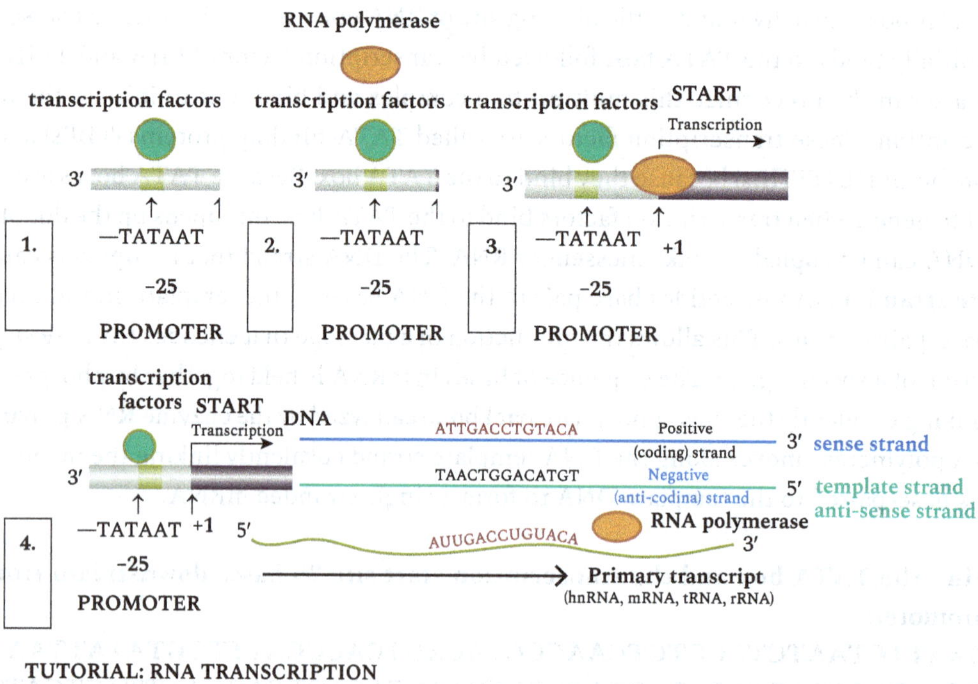

Figure 6.10

Tutorial: RNA transcription

5. RNA polymerase catalyzes the formation of a phosphodiester bond between the 5' phosphate of the incoming nucleotide and the 3'OH of the adjacent nucleotide.
6. Once transcription is complete the mRNA separates from the DNA template and the DNA helix reforms.
7. The mRNA can then serve as a template to direct the formation of a peptide—a string of amino acids whose sequence is determined by the genetic code of the mRNA.

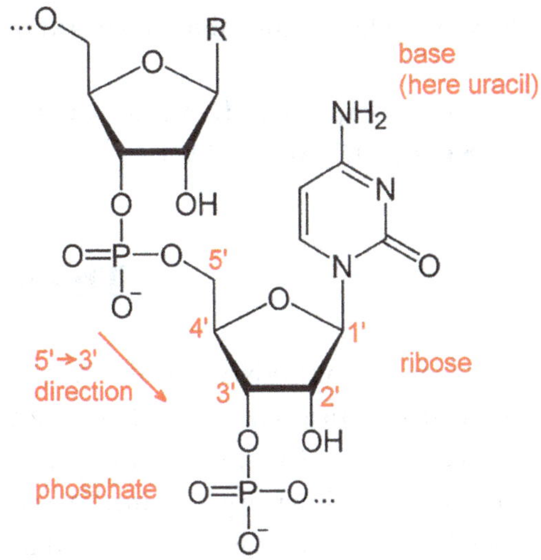

Figure 6.11

Messenger RNA cap

Processing the Message: Capping and Polyadenylation

In eukaryotic cells, this initial transcript must be modified chemically before it can travel from the nucleus to the cytoplasm. This involves the addition of a **5' cap** at the beginning of the transcript (see Figure 6.11). Shortly after transcription is completed in eukaryotes, a pre-mRNA's 5' end is modified by the addition of a 7-methylguanosine, also known as a 5' cap. The 5' capping modification is initiated by the addition of a GTP to the 5' terminal nucleotide of the pre-mRNA in reverse orientation followed by the addition of methyl groups to the G residue. 5' capping is essential for the production of functional mRNAs because the 5' cap is responsible for aligning the mRNA with the ribosome during translation.

In eukaryotes, **polyadenylation** further modifies pre-mRNAs during which a structure called the poly-A tail is added (see Figure 6.12). Signals for polyadenylation, which include several RNA sequence elements, are detected by a group of proteins that signal the addition of the poly-A tail (approximately 200 nucleotides in length). The poly-A tail helps the mRNA pass through the nuclear envelope to the cytoplasm. Let's see how this happens (see Figure 6.12).

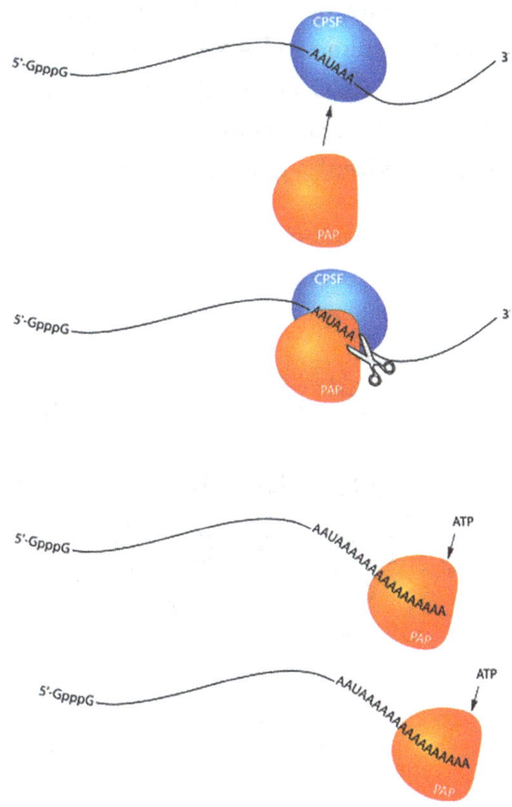

Figure 6.12

Addition of the poly-A tail

We want to learn more about how mRNA is processed in eukaryotic cells.

5. **Place a cap and poly-A tail on the following transcript:**
   5 GAUCUUAGCUUA 3'

The Genetic Code

So now we see how mRNA is made. But we still don't understand how it can function as a genetic code. We decide to go back to Dr. Nirenberg's lab to see if we can learn more about this secret code. When we arrive, Dr. Nirenberg is sitting in front of this metal instrument that looks nothing like a secret decoder. Dr. Nirenberg explains, "We cracked the code by putting in 3 base nucleotide segments to see which amino acid would be placed in a chain using a cell-free protein synthesizing system."

He drops the segment into the tube—it contains 5'UUU3' segment. This triplet nucleotide binds to the ribosome in the tube and adds the amino acid phenylalanine to the growing peptide chain. "AAHHH! Phenylalanine!" he exclaims. "This means that the triplet nucleotide UUU codes for phenylalanine, one of the 20 amino acids!" He tells us that he has already determined that CCC codes for proline and AAA codes for lysine. In fact, there are four triplets that code for proline: CCC, CCU, CCG, and CCA. Dr. Crick was right about the wobble!'

Now we are really confused—wobble? "Who's wobbling?" we ask. "The third base, of course," sighs Dr. Nirenberg. He pulls out a chart (see Figure 6.13). The experiments have shown that 3 bases of mRNA encode a single amino acid. Because there are four nucleotides, this means that there is a total of 64 combinations of triplet bases that can be made. Because there are only 20 amino acids, it appears that the code has a built-in redundancy—up to four triplets or codons—can specify a single amino acid. The variance is typically in the third base—it wobbles! We examine the code carefully. We can see it is redundant. "Does it have any punctuation?" we ask. "How does it know where to start and stop?" Dr. Nirenberg explains that there is a START codon that begins every message or coding region. This is AUG that codes for the amino acid methionine. There are also three stop codons that signal the end of the coding region—they are UAA, UAG, and UGA.

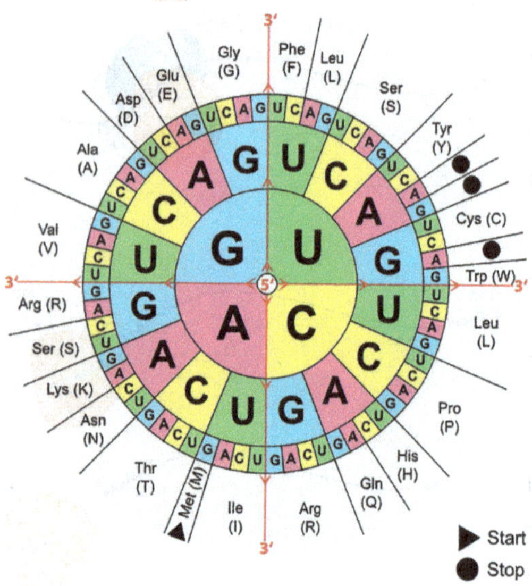

Figure 6.13

The genetic code

6. **Decode this mRNA: 5' AUGAAAUUUCCCUGA 3'**

This is remarkable! We can see that Dr. Nirenberg has worked very hard to unravel the genetic code in bacteria. "When are you going to try to crack the genetic code in humans?" we ask. He looks at us askance—"What are you talking about? This is the genetic code for humans!" We are somewhat incredulous. "But you are studying the code in bacteria, not humans. We know it is a lot of work—but no shortcuts—this is important research!"

Dr. Nirenberg motions that it is time for us to leave. "The genetic code is universal—it is the same for all forms of life!" he pronounces as he closes the door firmly behind us.

We are truly amazed—a universal code—and now we have seen how it works!

7. **Show all the codons for alanine**

> *The* New York Times *(1961 editorial) reported on Leder and Nirenberg's discovery by explaining that "the science of biology has reached a new frontier."*

Translating the Code

The next day—after we recover from our excitement about cracking the genetic code—we realize there's a lot we still don't know about this. How is it that the mRNA is actually decoded to place the right amino acid at the right position in the peptide chain?

Let's see how **translation** happens (see Figure 6.14).

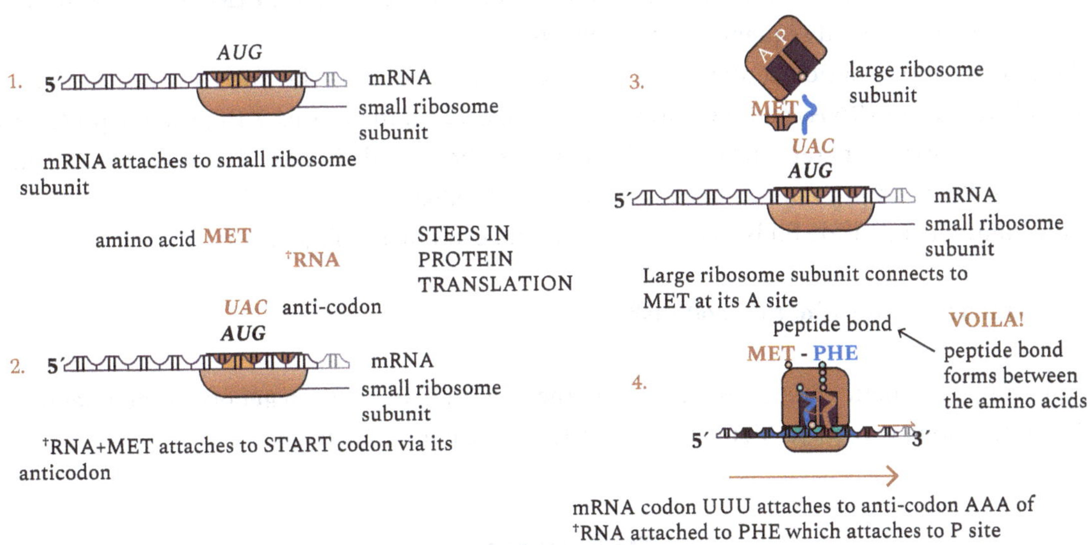

Figure 6.14

Tutorial: Protein translation—Part I

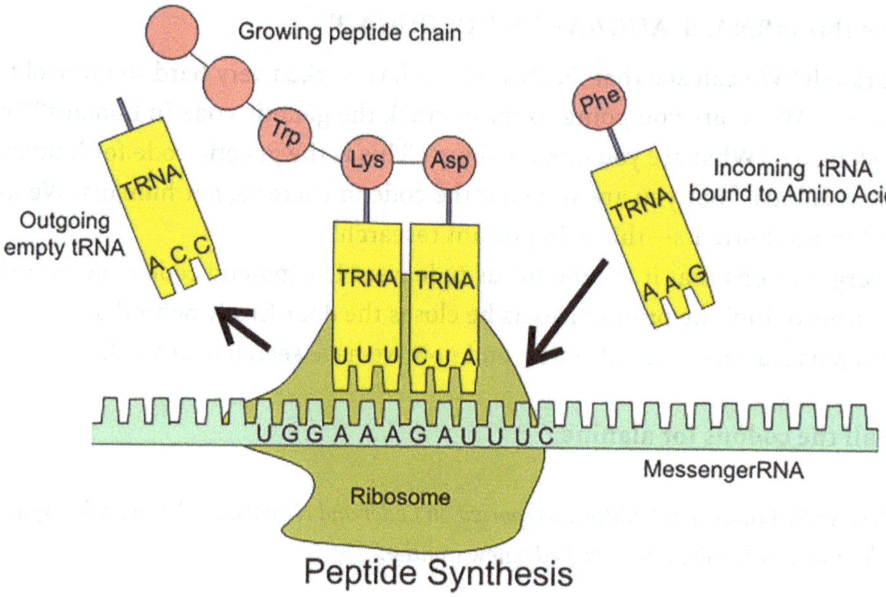

Figure 6.15

Tutorial: Protein translation—Part 2

8. **What is the tRNA for methionine?**

So now we realize that it is the transfer RNA that makes the magic—each tRNA is linked to a specific amino acid that is brought to the ribosome by base-pair bonding between the mRNA codon and the anticodon of the tRNA to which the amino acid is attached. It is the tRNA that "translates" the code to an amino acid sequence at the ribosome!

The process of translation continues as the ribosome slides along the mRNA to access new codons and attach new tRNAs and their attached amino acids at the P sites. After each peptide bond is formed, the tRNA separates from the ribosome and the peptide is extended as each new codon is accessed. Translation comes to an end when a STOP codon is reached—the complex dissociates and the completed peptide folds to generate a unique protein (see Figure 6.15).

9. **What are the termination codons?**

Deciphering the genetic code gives meaning to the relationship between genotype and phenotype. We've come a long way since Mendel—but realize we still have far to go.

Reference

Leavitt, Sarah, *Deciphering the Genetic Code: Marshall Nirenberg*. Bethesda, MD: Office of NIH History, 2004.

Figure Credits

Fig. 6.1: Source: https://commons.wikimedia.org/wiki/File:Dorothy_Hansine_Andersen.jpg

Fig. 6.2: U.S. Department of Energy, Genomic Science program, "Chromosome 7," https://public.ornl.gov/site/gallery/detail.cfm?id=372&topic=47&citation=&general=&restsection=. 2002.

Fig. 6.3: Copyright © Lbudd14 (CC BY-SA 3.0) at https://commons.wikimedia.org/wiki/File:CFTR_Protein_Panels.svg.

Fig. 6.5: Source: https://commons.wikimedia.org/wiki/File:Marshall_Nirenberg_performing_experiment.jpg

Fig. 6.6: Copyright © Sponk (CC BY-SA 3.0) at https://commons.wikimedia.org/wiki/File:Difference_DNA_RNA-EN.svg.

Fig. 6.7: Copyright © Rakhmanhakim (CC BY-SA 4.0) at https://commons.wikimedia.org/wiki/File:Rna-structure.jpg.

Fig. 6.8: Source: https://commons.wikimedia.org/wiki/File:Transcription.jpg

Fig. 6.9: Copyright © Apawnilation (CC BY-SA 4.0) at https://commons.wikimedia.org/wiki/File:Tatabox.svg.

Fig. 6.11: Source: https://commons.wikimedia.org/wiki/File:RNA_chemical_structure.png

Fig. 6.12: Copyright © Fdardel (CC BY-SA 3.0) at https://commons.wikimedia.org/wiki/File:Polyadenylation.svg?uselang=fr.

Fig. 6.13: Source: https://commons.wikimedia.org/wiki/File:Aminoacids_table.svg

Fig. 6.14: Source: https://commons.wikimedia.org/wiki/File:TRNA_ribosomes_diagram_en.svg

Fig. 6.15: Copyright © Boumphreyfr (CC BY-SA 3.0) at https://commons.wikimedia.org/wiki/File:Peptide_syn.png.

Chapter 7

Genes and Mutations: Changing the Genetic Code

The Causes of Mutations

Our studies of gene expression have shown us how the genetic code was cracked and how a 4 base sequence can encode almost limitless possibilities for genetic variation! We are pondering this wondrous system when we chance to pass by a large laboratory with an unusual sign outside (see Figure 7.1).

Figure 7.1

Caution sign

We decide to peer inside to see what's going on. We see a woman dressed in black moving quickly about the room. There are piles of black soot-like material everywhere, but in the corner we see a tube that is glowing faintly in the dark. "What is that?" we ask. "It's radium—and I have finally purified it from pitchblende after many years of extracting it from hundreds of pounds of material!" We congratulate her on her discovery as she introduces herself as Dr. Marie Curie (see Figure 7.2).

Figure 7.2

Portrait of Marie Curie (1867–1934)

We learn that radium has amazing properties due to the fact that it is radioactive. "It can even change the structure of DNA," she explains. "How can that happen?" we ask, very surprised that anything can alter the structure of the genetic material. She takes us to her office and pulls out her casebook.

Inside we see photographs of young children who appear to have burns on their bodies. Dr. Curie explains that these are the victims of the atomic bomb dropped in Hiroshima to end World War II. "What we didn't realize at the time was that radiation can penetrate the cells of the body to cause mutations—changes on the structure of DNA—that can have disastrous effects, causing inherited malformations and cancers such as leukemia" (see Figure 7.3).

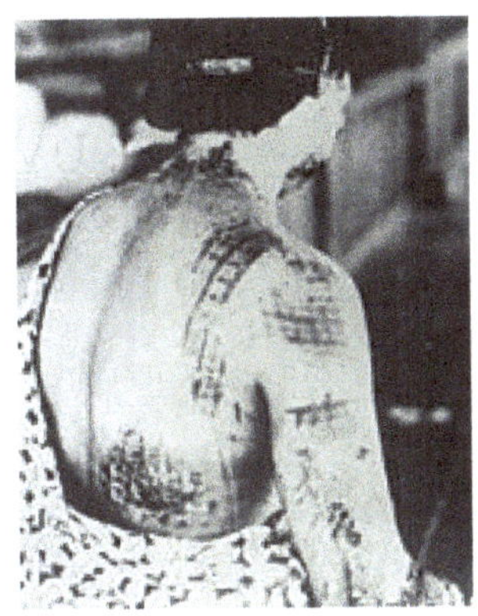

Figure 7.3

Woman burned by atomic bomb fallout, 1945

She explains how this can happen. "My friend, Dr. Hermann Muller, has recently discovered that X-rays cause gene mutations in fruit flies and suspects that the same can happen in human cells. These mutations can change the phenotype of the flies, for example, causing them to have white eyes rather than the customary red eyes—so it's easy to observe the effects of the X-rays using these organisms" (see Figure 7.4).

Radiation (X-rays and gamma rays) and chemicals that affect chromosomes and DNA are called mutagens. They can produce chromosomal breaks, rearrangements, and aneuploidies as well as altering the structure and function of individual genes (see Figure 7.5).

Figure 7.4

Laboratory where William Roentgen discovered X-rays in 1895.

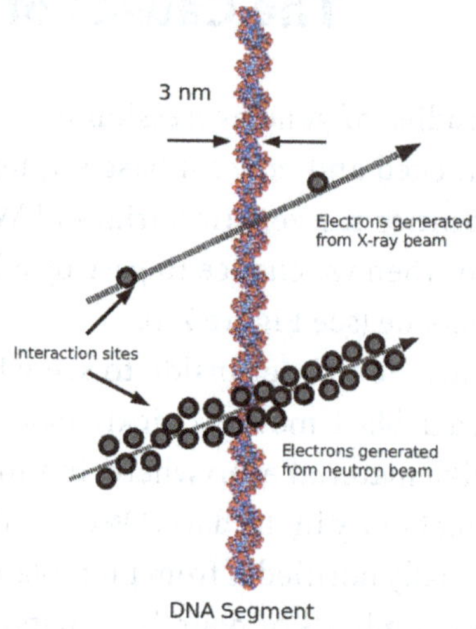

Figure 7.5

Mutagens can cause single- and double-strand DNA breaks

1. **What are the possible genetic consequences of DNA strand breaks caused by radiation?**

Even sunlight can cause mutations. Ultraviolet radiations with wavelength above 260 nm are absorbed strongly by the bases in DNA, producing pyrimidine dimers, which can cause errors in replication if left uncorrected (see Figure 7.6).

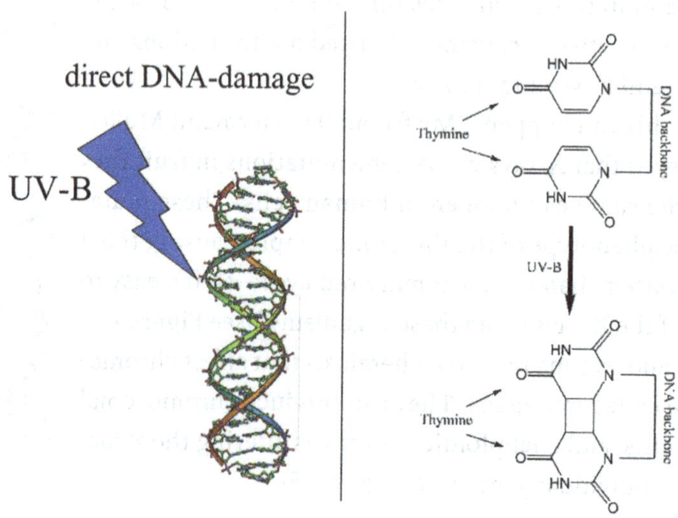

Figure 7.6

Ultraviolet radiation exposure can cause adjacent thymine bases to dimerize

We want to learn more about how mutations occur (see Figure 7.7A).

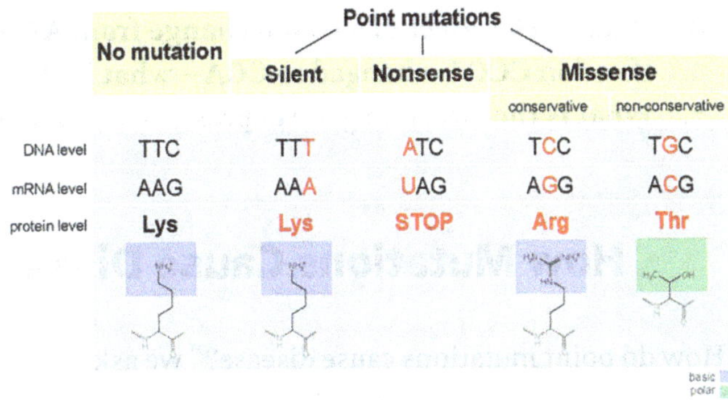

Figure 7.7A

Types of Mutations

At the level of individual genes, mutagens can cause changes in nucleotide sequence that may alter the genetic code. These changes include **point mutations** that affect only a single base:

- **Substitution**—one base is exchanged for another
- **Insertion**—one base is added
- **Deletion**—one base is removed

Point insertions and deletions are called **frameshift** because they alter the reading of the triplet codons from the point of insertion or deletion all the way to the end of the coding region (see Figure 7.7B).

2. **What is the effect of a point mutation that changes the first ATG in the coding region to TTG?**

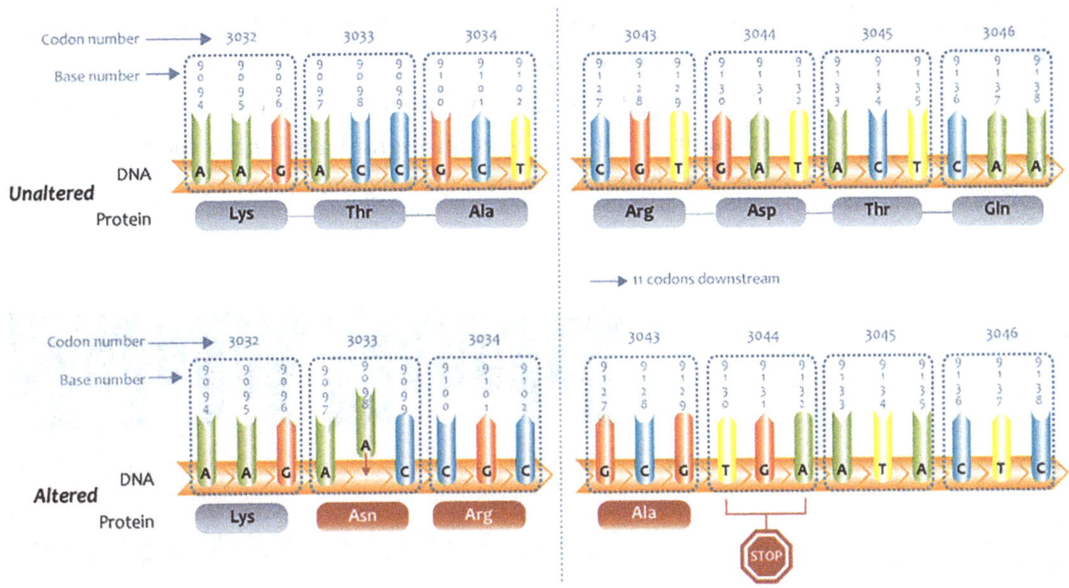

Figure 7.7B

3. **What is the effect of a codon change from AGA to UGA?**
4. **If codon CCC is changed to CCA—what is the effect on gene expression?**
5. **What is the effect on gene expression if codon CAU is changed to codon CAG?**

How Mutations Cause Disease: Sickle Cell Anemia

"How do point mutations cause disease?" we ask. Dr. Curie sends us to the laboratory of Dr. Linus Pauling who is busy at the bench with some test tubes and reagent bottles. We ask him how a single base chain in the billions of bases in the human genome can possibly cause a serious genetic disorder. "Well, look at sickle cell disease. It can be fatal and it is caused by a single base change!" he asserts confidently. "Take a look at this cell" (see Figure 7.8).

These are from a patient with sickle cell disease. The hemoglobin protein is abnormal and distorts the structure of the red blood cell, making it look like a sickle.

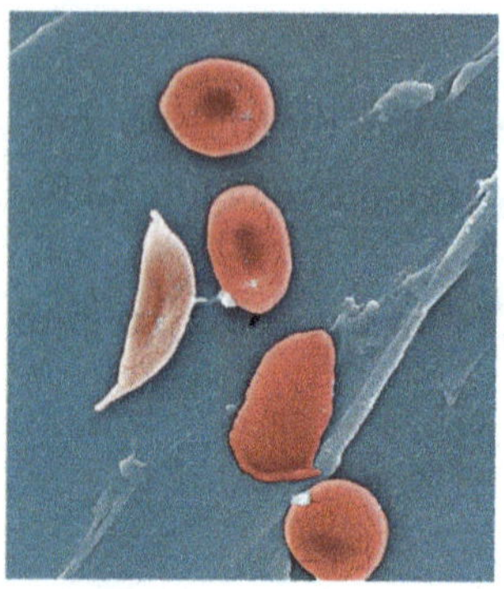

Figure 7.8

Red blood cells from a patient with sickle cell disease

"This happens as a result of only one base change in DNA?" we ask, incredulous. "Oh yes, I'll show you how this happens." He shows us an image from a paper he has just published (see Figure 7.9). He explains that proteins travel in an electric field through a gel matrix based on their biochemical properties. There are two bands of hemoglobin from individuals who are heterozygous for this recessive disease; one-half of the hemoglobin has the normal properties and the other half is biochemically different. You can also see that the hemoglobin from patients with sickle cell disease is all found in the band that migrates to the abnormal position in the gel.

"How could this happen?" we ask. "You have to look at the DNA" (see Figure 7.10). "Dr. Vernon Ingram and I have found that a single base-pair change in the beta globin gene causes a change in one amino

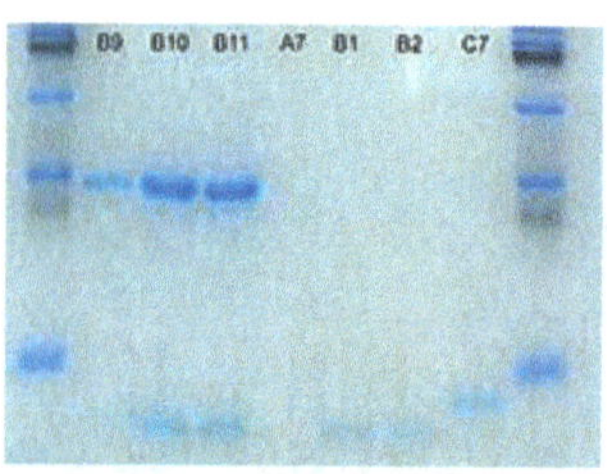

Figure 7.9

Protein electrophoresis of normal hemoglobin and hemoglobin from patients with sickle cell trait or disease

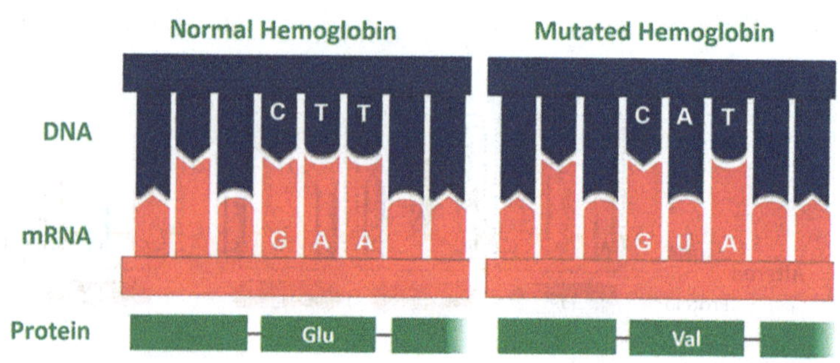

Figure 7.10

Mutation responsible for sickle cell disease

acid of the protein—from glutamic acid to valine." This amino acid substitution causes the protein to have an abnormal structure that causes anemia, blot clots, and internal bleeding. The disease can be fatal.

6. **How can a missense mutation—such as in sickle cell disease—result in a protein that has an abnormal structure?**

Some of these mutations are lethal or cause serious disease, such as cystic fibrosis and sickle cell disease. Many of these point mutations that cause genetic disorders occur as a result of errors in DNA replication or crossing over.

7. **What will be the consequence if a single base is deleted from the coding region of a gene?**

DNA Repair Defects

DNA mutations can also result from defects in cell processes that are designed to protect DNA from damage. We are very surprised to learn that these cellular processes can go so wrong! For example, nucleotide excision repair is an important repair process that excises pyrimidine dimers caused by exposure to ultraviolet light and then fills in the gap by synthesizing new replacement DNA (see Figure 7.11).

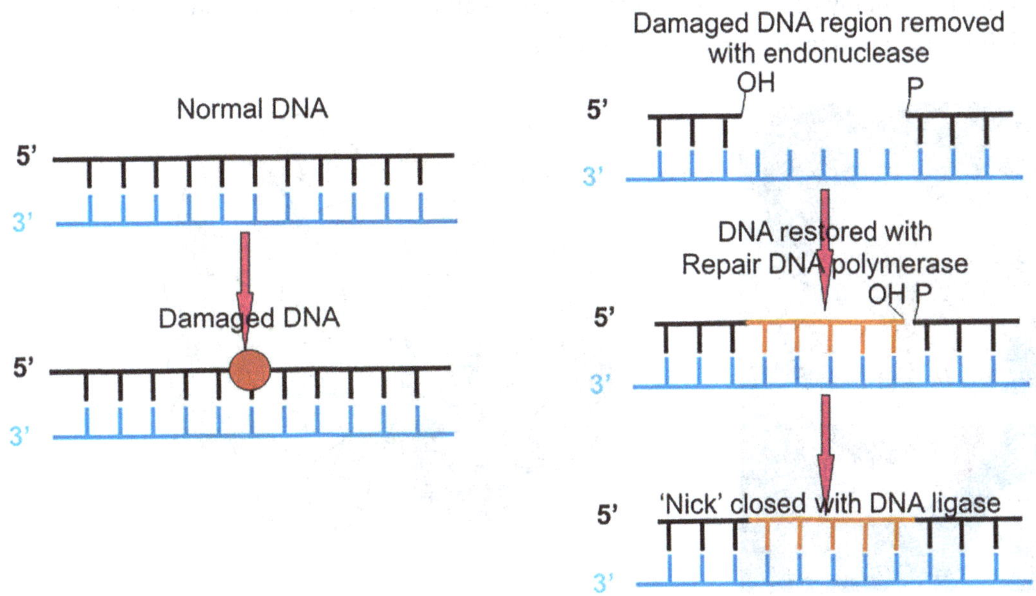

Figure 7.11

DNA excision repair

Defects in this repair process result in an inherited genetic disorder called Xeroderma pigmentosum (XP) resulting in skin discoloration and multiple tumors on exposure to UV light that may cause a serious skin cancer called melanoma (see Figure 7.12).

Children with XP have defects in the nucleotide excision repair genes (NER) that code for proteins that normally repair DNA damage caused by exposure to ultraviolet radiation in sunlight. As a consequence, the unrepaired DNA mutations can cause skin cancers that are sometimes fatal. Diseases such as XP that affect the ability of the cell to repair DNA highlight the importance of these cellular repair mechanisms in maintaining normal cell functions.

Another important mechanism of DNA repair is called proofreading. Many DNA polymerases can detect errors in base-pair formation during replication and remove the incorrect base using a 3' to 5' exonuclease activity and then inserting the correct base. Without the proofreading activity of these enzymes, the mutation rate would be much higher!

The Spectrum of Mutations: Hemoglobin

"Are all mutations harmful?" we ask. Dr. Pauling assures us that this is not the case. "Without mutation, the genome would have no capacity to change. Genetic evolution would come to a standstill—in fact, it never would have occurred in the first place. We'd all look like bacteria!" he laughs and then frowns slightly as he realizes we don't really appreciate his attempt at humor. "So, mutation is a good thing," we propose. "Usually not!" he says emphatically. "Look at hemoglobin. I've been studying it all my life and you wouldn't believe all the things that can go wrong!" He invites us back into the lab to take a closer look (see Figure 7.13).

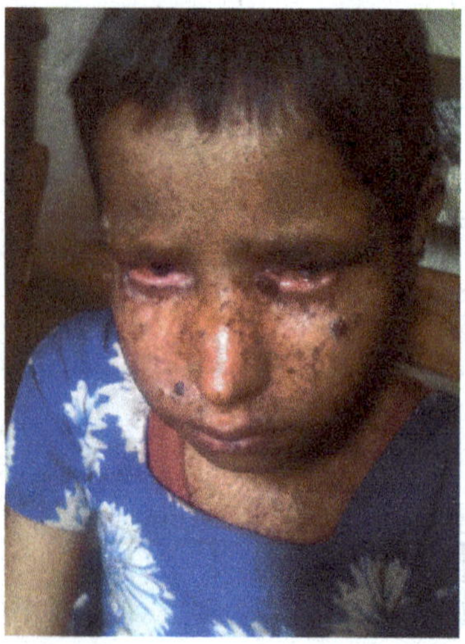

Figure 7.12

Young girl with Xeroderma pigmentosum

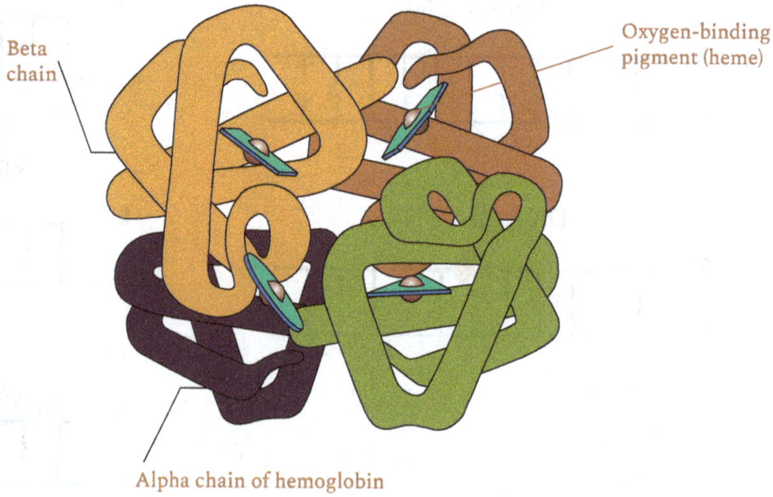

Figure 7.13

Hemoglobin

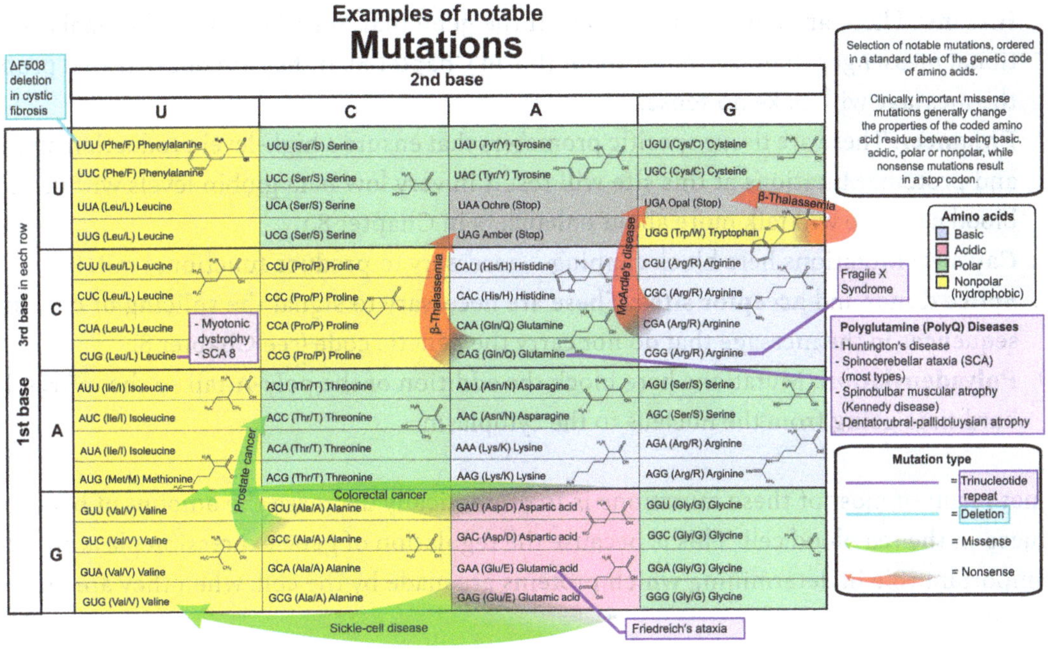

Figure 7.14

Mutations identified in the hemoglobin BETA gene

Human hemoglobin is a tetramer—it has four protein subunits—two alpha globin and two beta globin chains. The alpha and beta subunits are encoded by different genes. Hemoglobin binds oxygen at the heme group and transports it to all the cells of the body and then transports CO_2 back to the lungs where it is exhaled.

Mutations in the hemoglobin genes are the most common human genetic disorders. Mutations that disrupt the heme binding site are lethal because oxygen is essential to life. But there are many forms of anemia that result from less serious changes in these genes. We've already seen how a single base change in DNA results in sickle cell disease. Dr. Pauling shows us some other hemoglobin disorders that result from different mutations in the beta globin gene (see Figure 7.14).

We are stunned by all the locations in the beta globin gene that contain mutations identified in patients with beta thalassemia! Let's examine these in closer detail:

1. **Promoter:** The canonical TATA box is altered—without a functional promoter, no mRNA or protein is made.
2. **Exons:** These are the regions of the gene that encode the protein—they contain the genetic code. Mutations here can alter the amino acid sequence of the protein affecting the structure and function of the hemoglobin protein.

3. **Introns:** These are noncoding regions of the gene that must be removed to make a functional messenger RNA (see more about this in Chapter 8). If they are not removed properly, the message will make no sense.
4. **Enhancer:** These are tissue specific promoters that ensure a high-level production of mRNA and protein. Mutations at this site will result in very low beta globin levels within the red blood cell. (We will talk more about enhancers in Chapter 8.)
5. **Cap site:** Mutations here block capping—necessary to produce functional mRNA.

6/7/8. **Splice donor** and **acceptor sites:** These are necessary to signal the splicing or cutting out sequences in the message that do not carry the genetic code (see Chapter 8).

9. **Polyadenylation:** Mutations here block the addition of the poly-A tail so the mRNA has a hard time going from the nucleus to the cytoplasm.

The net result of most of these mutations is to dramatically decrease the amount of beta globin produced in the red blood cell. This is because the regulation of gene expression plays an incredibly important role in determining which proteins are made by the cell, when they are made and how much.

8. **What is the consequence on gene expression if the TATA box sequence is changed from TATA to CATA?**
9. **What will happen to gene expression if the polyadenylation signal sequence is altered?**

We want to learn more about gene regulation and disorders of hemoglobin. We head straight for Chapter 8!

Figure Credits

Fig. 7.1: Source: https://commons.wikimedia.org/wiki/File:Radio_waves_hazard_symbol.svg
Fig. 7.2: Copyright © Wellcome Library (CC BY 4.0) at https://commons.wikimedia.org/wiki/File:Portrait_of_Marie_Curie_(1867_-_1934),_Polish_chemist_Wellcome_M0004624.jpg.
Fig. 7.3: Source: https://commons.wikimedia.org/wiki/File:The_patient%27s_skin_is_burned_in_a_pattern_corresponding_to_the_dark_portions_of_a_kimono_-_NARA_-_519686.jpg
Fig. 7.4: Source: https://commons.wikimedia.org/wiki/File:Room_where_R%C3%B6ntgen_found_x-rays.jpg
Fig. 7.5: Source: https://commons.wikimedia.org/wiki/File:DNA-Interaction.png
Fig. 7.6: Source: https://commons.wikimedia.org/wiki/File:Direct_DNA_damage.png
Fig. 7.7a: Copyright © Jonsta247 (CC BY-SA 4.0) at https://commons.wikimedia.org/wiki/File:Point_mutations-en.png.
Fig. 7.7b: Copyright © Genomics Education Programme (CC BY 2.0) at https://commons.wikimedia.org/wiki/File:Frameshift_duplication_(13062836963).jpg.
Fig. 7.8: Copyright © OpenStax College (CC BY 3.0) at https://commons.wikimedia.org/wiki/File:1911_Sickle_Cells.jpg.
Fig. 7.9: Copyright © Marieke Kuijjer (CC BY-SA 2.0) at https://commons.wikimedia.org/wiki/File:Sds-page_electrophoresis.jpg.

Fig. 7.10: Copyright © (CC BY-SA 4.0) at https://commons.wikimedia.org/wiki/File:Point-Mutation-Sickle-Cell-Normal_and_Mutated-Hemoglobin.png.
Fig. 7.11: Copyright © Boumphreyfr (CC BY-SA 3.0) at https://commons.wikimedia.org/wiki/File:Dna_repair.png.
Fig. 7.12: Copyright © Himynameislax (CC BY-SA 3.0) at https://commons.wikimedia.org/wiki/File:Child_suffering_from_Xeroderma_Pigmentosum_in_Rukum,Nepal.jpg.
Fig. 7.13: Source: https://commons.wikimedia.org/wiki/File:Hemoglobin_structure.JPG
Fig. 7.14: Source: https://commons.wikimedia.org/wiki/File:Notable_mutations.svg

Chapter 8

Regulation of Gene Expression

Figure 8.1

Which way to Dr. Lwoff's lab?

The Bacterial Operon

We are fascinated by the idea that genes follow directions! We thought directions only apply to traffic signals and maps telling us where to go—why is this important for genes? We are totally confused and decide to head directly to the lab of Dr. Andre Lwoff, that is, if we can find it (please see Figure 8.1)! After a long day of traveling—mostly aimlessly—we arrive at our destination—the Pasteur Institute. We go inside and Dr. Lwoff is busy behind the bench pouring flasks of discolored liquid onto petri dishes.

"We came here to learn about gene regulation," we ask, somewhat skeptical about receiving a relevant explanation. "I am studying cultures of bacteria and how genes are turned on and off," he says matter-of-factly. We nod, somewhat relieved that perhaps we have come to the right place after all. "Come up to 'le grenier'—I will show you more." "Isn't that the attic?" we ask. "Yes, that is where they put me—but you will be surprised at what I've done with the place!" We climb the steep steps to a small, very warm laboratory and notice many culture dishes stacked in neat rows. "What I have discovered" he explains, "is that there are two kinds of genes: genes that produce proteins by coding for mRNA that is then translated to make proteins, and genes that turn protein coding genes on and off." These are regulatory genes. We decide to take a closer look (see Figure 8.2).

We learn that the **operon** is a genetic unit found in bacteria that is an important model for studying gene regulation mechanisms. The operon consists of structural genes—the genes that encode proteins—and a regulatory segment that determines when the protein coding genes are turned on or off. The first regulator element is the promoter. This is the binding site for RNA polymerase. Once RNA polymerase binds to the **promoter**, it can transcribe the adjacent structural genes to make mRNA and proteins needed by the cell.

The operon also contains a regulatory element that acts as a molecular traffic signal that can allow or block the polymerase from transcribing the structural genes. This is called the **operator**. The operator can turn off gene expression (red light) when it binds a protein called the **repressor**. The repressor does just that—it represses transcription. When the repressor is NOT attached to

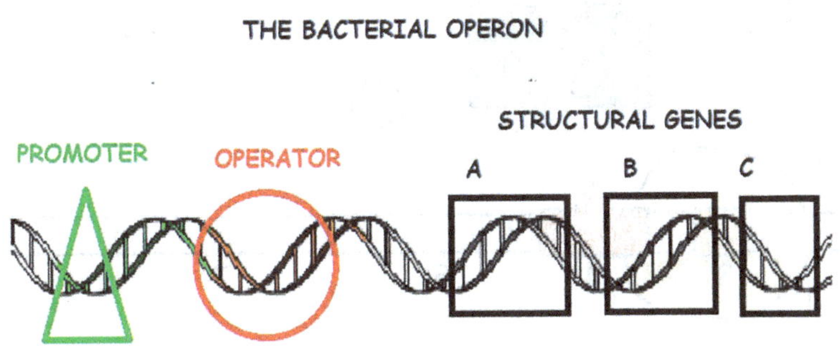

Figure 8.2

A bacterial operon

the operator (green light) the RNA polymerase can travel through the molecular intersection and transcribe the structural genes.

1. **Where does RNA polymerase bind to the operon?**
2. **Where does the repressor bind to the operon?**

Inducible Gene Regulation: The *lac* Operon

We check out an operon to see how it works (see Figure 8.3). We see that RNA polymerase (1-yellow) binds to the promoter (3-brown) but can't get through to transcribe the structural genes (6, 7, 8) because the repressor (2-green) is bound to the operator (4-red) in the upper panel.

In the lower panel, the repressor is not bound to the operator, so the RNA polymerase can bind to the promoter and transcribe mRNA. "What happened?" we ask. Dr. Lwoff explains that this type of promoter is **inducible**—meaning that when an inducer binds to the repressor, the repressor can

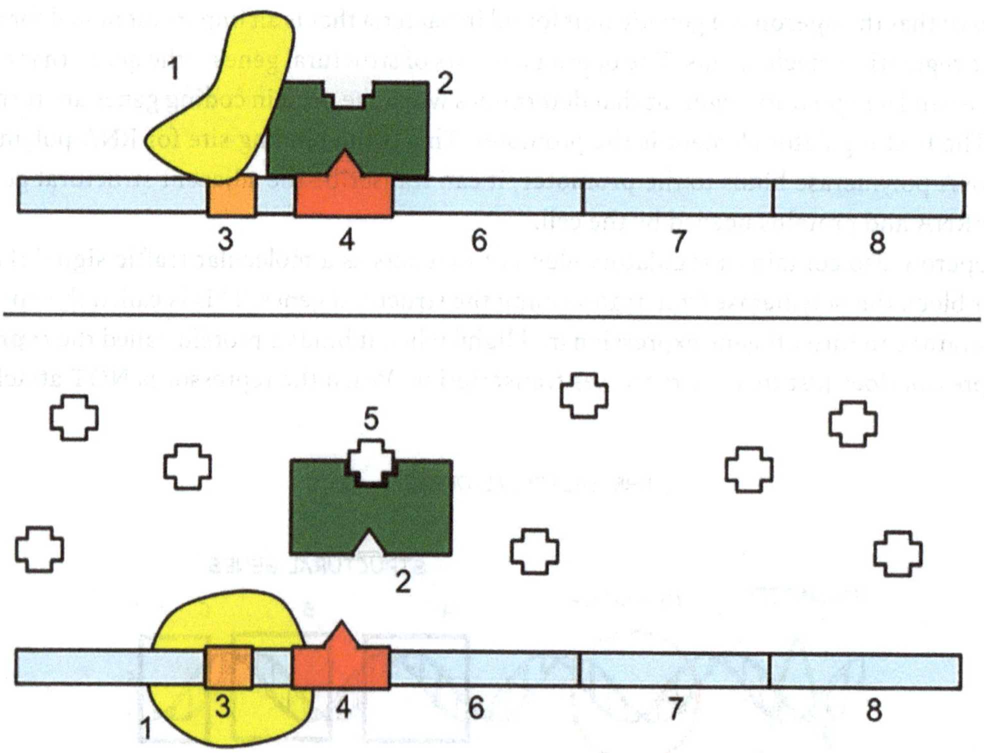

Figure 8.3

The *lac* operon

no longer attach to the operator because its structure is changed—so transcription is induced. "Clever, isn't it?" he adds.

3. **True or false: If the repressor is bound to the operator, transcription cannot occur.**
4. **True or false: In an inducible system, the inducer inactivates the repressor.**
5. **True or false: The function of the inducer is to turn on transcription.**

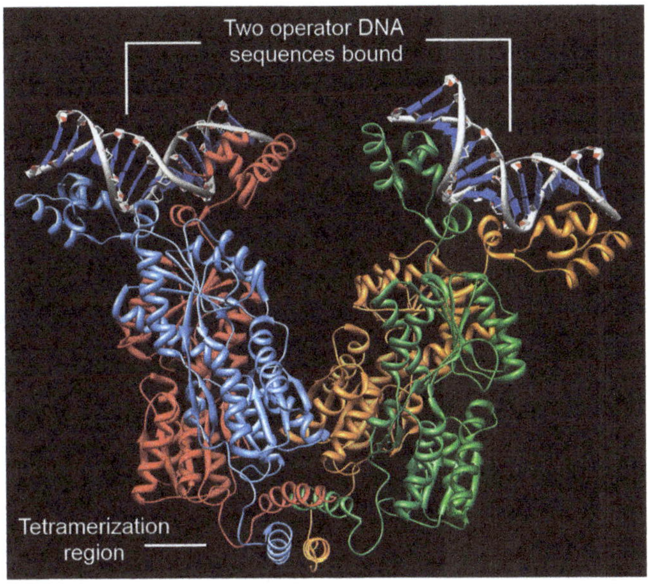

Figure 8.4

The *lac* repressor protein

"Why go to all this trouble?" we ask. "Why do bacteria need repressors?" Dr. Lwoff explains that some proteins are not always needed by the cell—so they are only made when they are needed. An important example is the ***lac* operon**. This operon contains the genes for metabolizing the sugar lactose to obtain energy. When lactose is present in the culture medium, this sugar acts as an **inducer** to turn on the genes needed for its digestion. When lactose is not around, the repressor sits on the operator, blocking the production of unwanted, unneeded proteins (see Figure 8.4).

Repressible Gene Regulation: The *trp* Operon

There is another kind of operon called **repressible**. In this kind of operon, the **repressor** by itself is inactive and can't bind the operator unless a co-repressor binds to it. So, the green light for transcription is usually on. A good example of a repressible operon is the ***trp* operon** (see Figure 8.5). This operon contains the genes required to synthesize the amino acid tryptophan. The genes are usually turned on, because the cell needs this amino acid to make proteins. But if the level of tryptophan rises too high in the cell, the excess tryptophan binds to the inactive repressor—changing its structure so it can bind to the operator to turn off transcription. Tryptophan is a co-repressor that activates the repressor to control the level of amino acid in the cell.

6. **Is the trp repressor active or inactive in the absence of the co-repressor?**
7. **At low levels of tryptophan is the trp operon turned on or off?**
8. **At high levels of tryptophan is the trp operon turned on or off?**

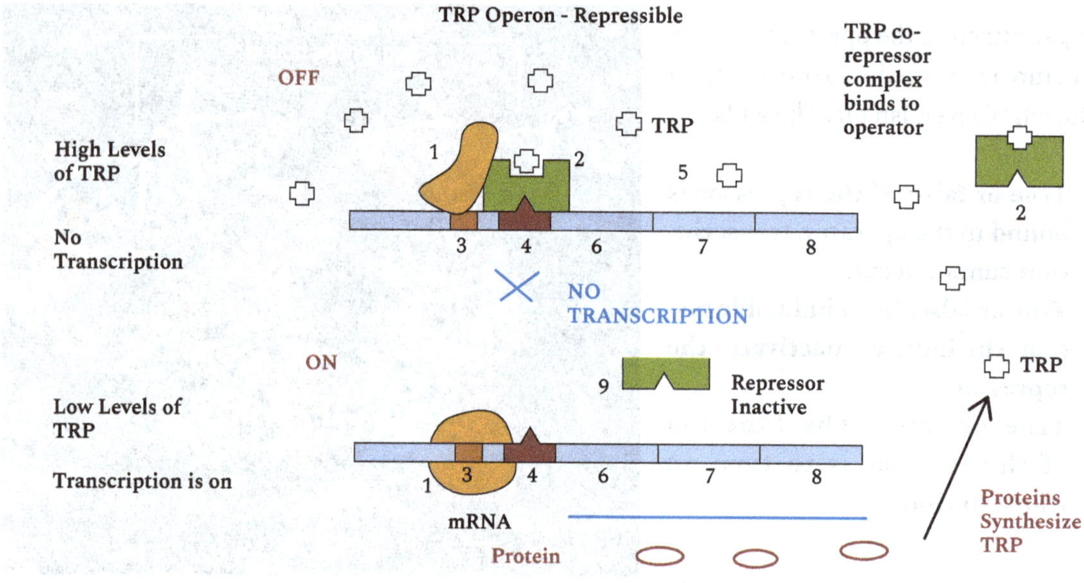

Figure 8.5

The *trp* operon

This type of gene regulation is called **feedback control**. There are similarities between this type of bacterial gene regulation and the regulatory circuitry that regulates gene expression in higher forms of life.

Gene Regulation in Eukaryotic Cells

Regulation starts with the gene—the DNA itself (see Figure 8.6). Because DNA is found in the cell as highly coiled chromatin, the DNA must be exposed so that it will be accessible to the enzymes that carry out transcription. Posttranscriptional processing of newly synthesized pre-mRNA is a second level of control. The RNA must then successfully exit the nucleus and travel to the ribosome so that translation can occur. Finally, the longevity of the mRNA and the activity of the final protein product all represent levels where gene expression can be regulated in sophisticated multicellular systems. Each level of control must be sensitive to regulatory feedback to maintain homeostasis in the cells, tissues, and organ systems of the body (see Figure 8.7).

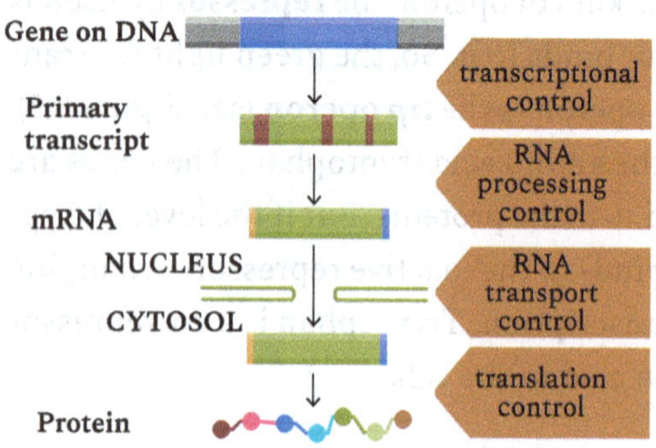

Figure 8.6

Levels of regulatory control of gene expression in eukaryotic cells

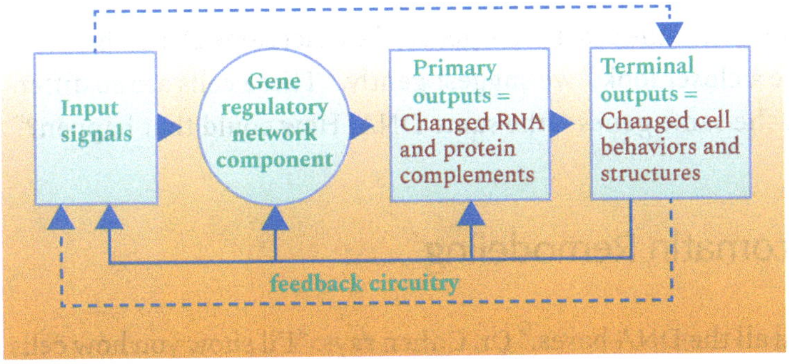

Figure 8.7

Gene feedback circuitry

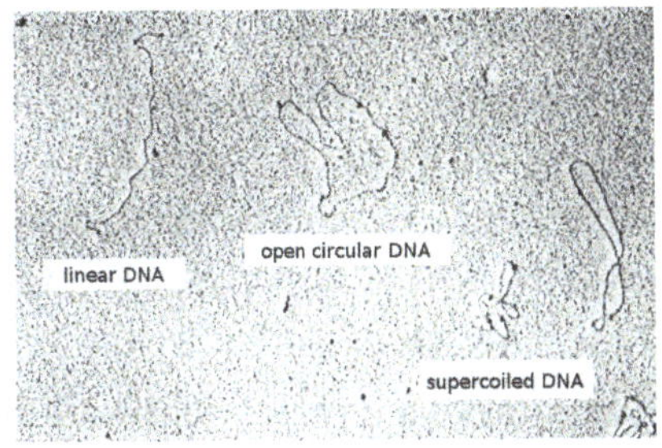

Figure 8.8

DNA used in gene cloning

We leave "le grenier" very impressed with the notion that a cell can regulate the amount of protein it produces. "We wonder if this happens in humans, too?" we ask. "You'll have to see Dr. Cohen for that—he has a DNA factory with lots of specimens! Human DNA, too!"

We're very anxious to take a closer look at some human DNA so we race over to Dr. Stanley Cohen's lab. He shows us several samples of DNA under the electron microscope (see Figure 8.8).

"We've been putting human DNA into small DNA circles called **plasmids**—these can be cultured to make millions of copies of the DNA we want to study," Dr. Cohen explains. "From these studies, we have found that humans and other multicellular organisms contain DNA regulatory regions that control gene expression. For example, look at this skin cell—then look at this nerve cell—they look very different, don't they?" (see Figure 8.9).

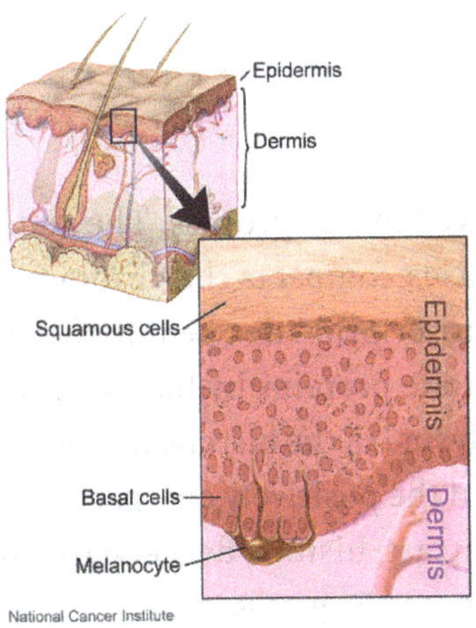

Figure 8.9A

Skin cell

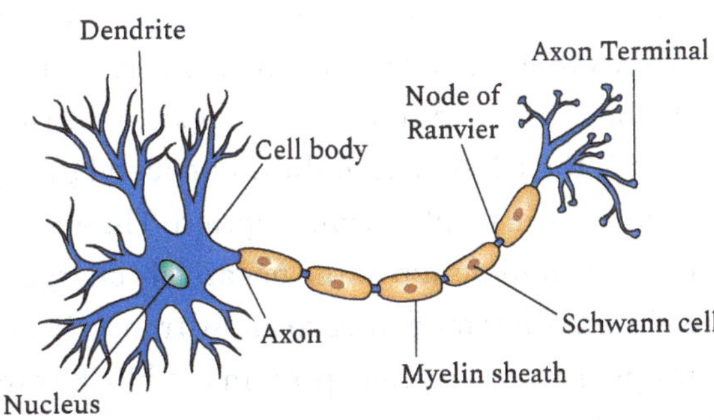

Figure 8.9B

Nerve cell

"Yes, of course," we respond. "Well they have the exact same genes, the exact same DNA!" he states confidently. "Perhaps ***you*** should take a closer look," we suggest gently. "These cells are so different that they could not possibly have the same genes—the same DNA! How could that happen?"

Chromatin Remodeling

"I *have* taken a *very close look*—studied all the DNA bases," Dr. Cohen says. "I'll show you how cells with the same genes look very different and do very different things."

He shows us images of chromosomes (see Figure 8.10). Apparently, this is where gene regulation begins. We see that negatively charged DNA is tightly bound to basic, positively charged histone proteins and cannot be transcribed to make mRNA unless the chromatin is opened up—this is called **chromatin remodeling.** Open regions of chromosomes—called **euchromatin**—actively transcribe mRNA. The openness of a chromosomal region is controlled in part by methylation. The more methylated the region, the less active the genes in that segment.

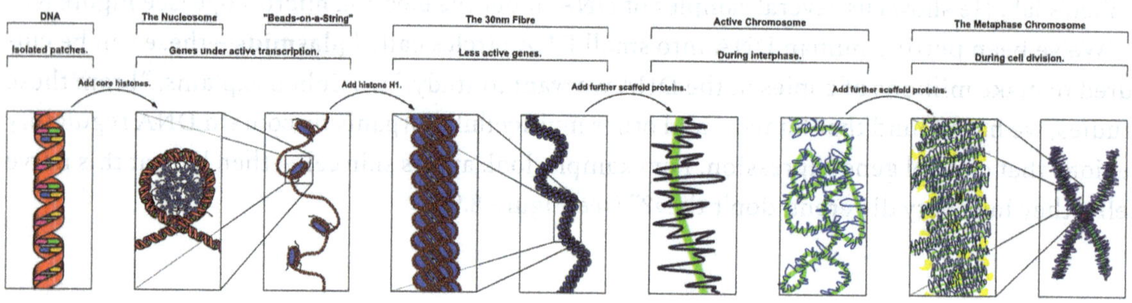

Figure 8.10

Chromatin structure

There are several important types of enzymes that are involved in this process. The addition of methyl groups to histone proteins by enzymes called methylases compacts the chromatin more tightly to block transcription or, at other sites, can activate transcription by opening the chromation to expose the DNA. The addition of acetyl groups to histone proteins by histone acetylases opens the chromatin to allow transcription. The acetylation of lysine in the histone proteins relaxes the electrostatic interaction of the negatively charged DNA and the positively charged histones to promote chromatin remodeling to allow transcription. In contrast, histone deacetylases remove acetyl groups from the histone proteins to block transcription (see Figure 8.11).

Biochemical modifications of DNA also control gene expression. For example, when CpG dinucleotides in DNA are methylated to form 5-methyl cytosone, DNA transcription is blocked. Groups

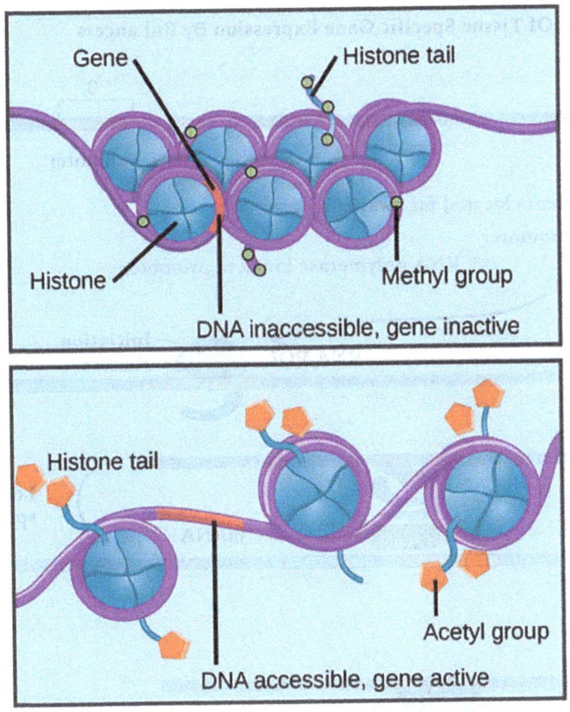

Figure 8.11

Chromatin remodeling

of CpG dinuleotides are often located near promoters to control their accessibility to transcription initiation factors and RNA polymerase (see Figure 8.12).

Regulation of Transcription

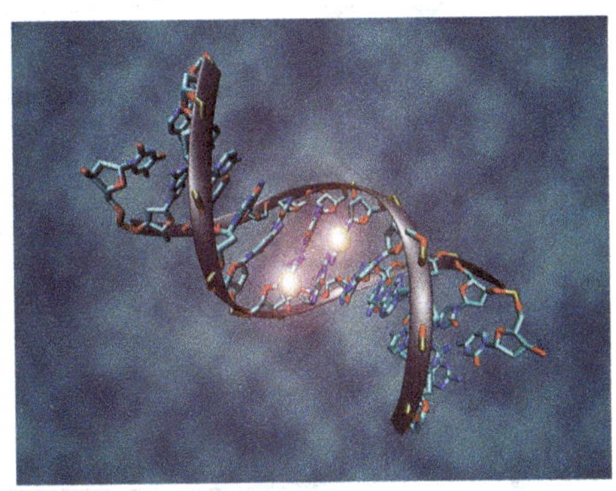

Figure 8.12

DNA methylation: Bright spots indicate the position of the methyl groups

To achieve high level activation of tissue specific genes, highly specialized control elements are required. These are called **enhancers**. Enhancers are tissue-specific promoters that can be activated by proteins called **activators**. The activator proteins are only found in specialized cells. The activators bind to the **enhancers** that causes a large increase in the amount of mRNA transcribed by the gene regulated by the enhancer. There are also **silencer** sequences in DNA that can bind to repressor proteins to down regulate the amount of mRNA produced by a specific gene. Let's take a closer look at how this works (see Figure 8.13).

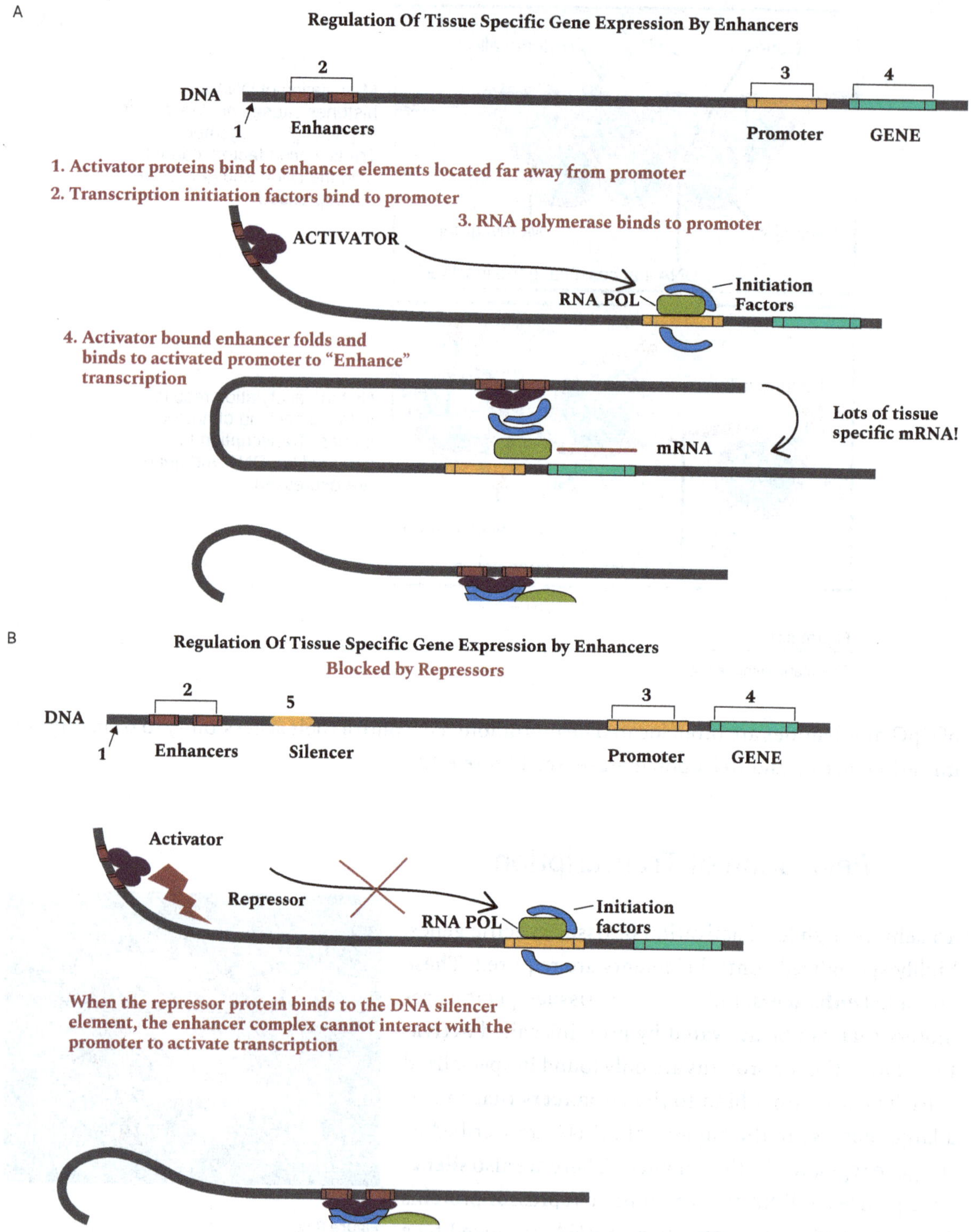

Figures 8.13A,B

Tutorial: Gene regulation by enhancers

9. **What regulatory unit in DNA binds to activator proteins?**
10. **True or false: The silencer blocks transcription enhancer function only when bound to a repressor protein.**

Enhancers and silencers (insulators) coordinately regulate gene expression. We see that when the enhancer is attached to activator proteins, it folds over and interacts with the promoter to stabilize the open template and enhance transcription by RNA polymerase. Repressor-silencer interactions destabilize the association of the enhancer with the promoter to decrease transcription.

Split Genes

"A close look at gene structure has also revealed a very surprising observation—many protein coding genes in higher organisms contain lots of noncoding regions," Dr. Cohen tells us. "For an explanation, you'll have to go and visit Dr. Chambon." We thank Dr. Cohen and we're on our way.

When we meet Dr. Pierre Chambon, he is carrying a huge pair of scissors. "What are you doing with those?" we ask. "So you will understand how they work in the cell," he explains, somewhat cryptically. "Many genes have only small pieces of coding information—called **exons**—that are interspersed among large noncoding segment called **introns**. I discovered that the cell uses molecular scissors to cut out the noncoding introns and paste together the exons to make a finished mRNA that can then code for protein during translation. This is called **splicing**."

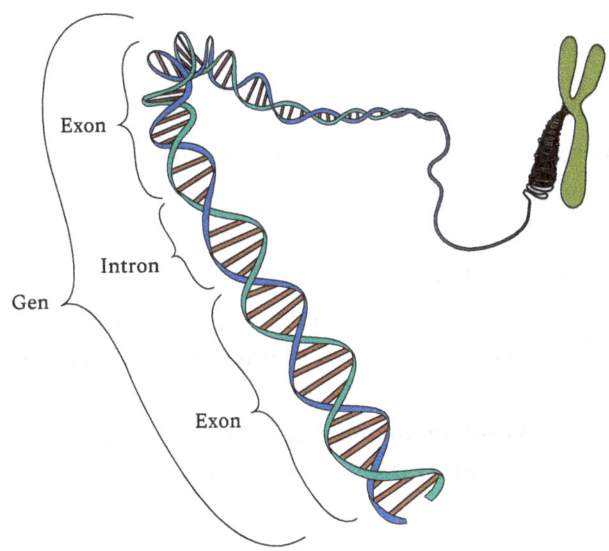

Figure 8.14

Split genes

Dr. Chambon invites us to take a closer look (see Figure 8.14).

Dr. Chambon shows us a close-up of a gene whose pre-messenger RNA is about to be spliced (see Figure 8.15).

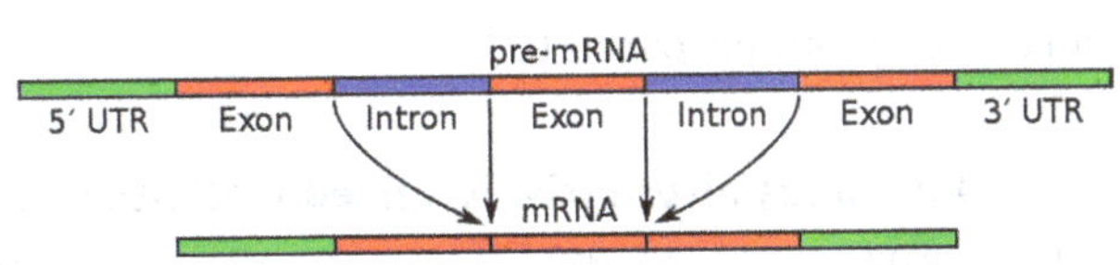

Figure 8.15

Introns and exons

The exons that contain the codons used in protein translation are separated by noncoding introns. When the gene is transcribed, the initial RNA produced (sometimes called the **primary transcript**) contains both introns and exons. Then this primary transcript

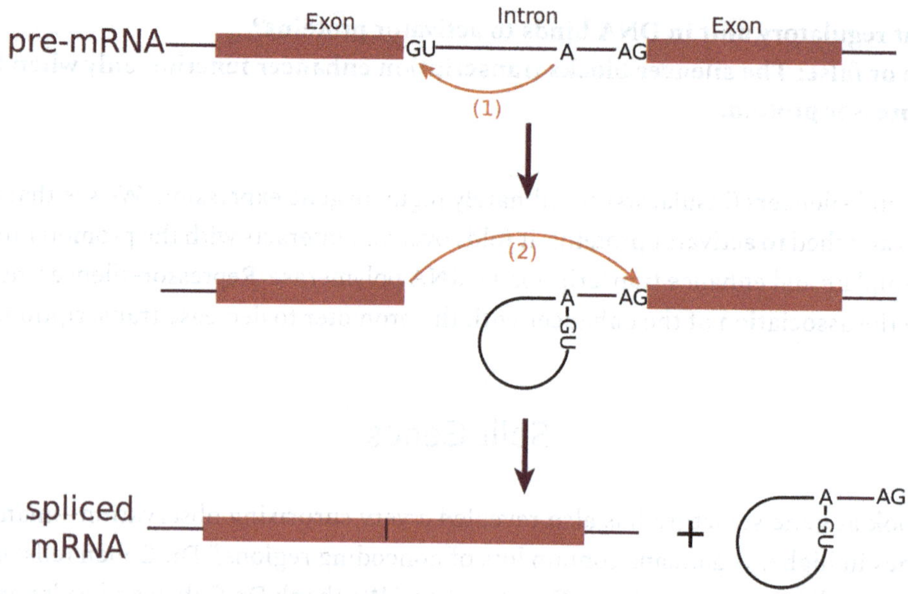

Figure 8.16

Tutorial: Splicing

is spliced—the introns are precisely excised—and the exons are fused to make a mature mRNA. This mRNA now contains the entire coding region fused together in the genetic code that specifies the sequence of amino acids in the protein. Let's see how this happens (see Figure 8.16).

We see that pre-messenger RNA splicing to remove noncoding introns is carried out in a series of steps by an elaborate complex of proteins and small RNAs called SNURPS (small nuclear ribonucleoproteins). This ribonucleoprotein complex is called the **spliceosome** (see Figure 8.17).

11. **Which segments of a split gene contain coding information?**
12. **Why must the introns be removed from pre-messenger RNA?**

We can see that mRNA splicing is an incredibly precise process! "But why does the cell go to all that trouble—putting in useless, noncoding segments in between coding regions—just to cut them out of the mRNA later?" "Aha!" exclaims Dr. Chambon, waving his scissors in the air. "It looks like split genes can explain how the genome of complex species has evolved over time." We are slightly incredulous, but prepared to listen.

13. **How many alternatively spiced mRNAs could be produced from this gene:**
14. **exon1 ______ exon2 ______ exon3 ______ exon4**

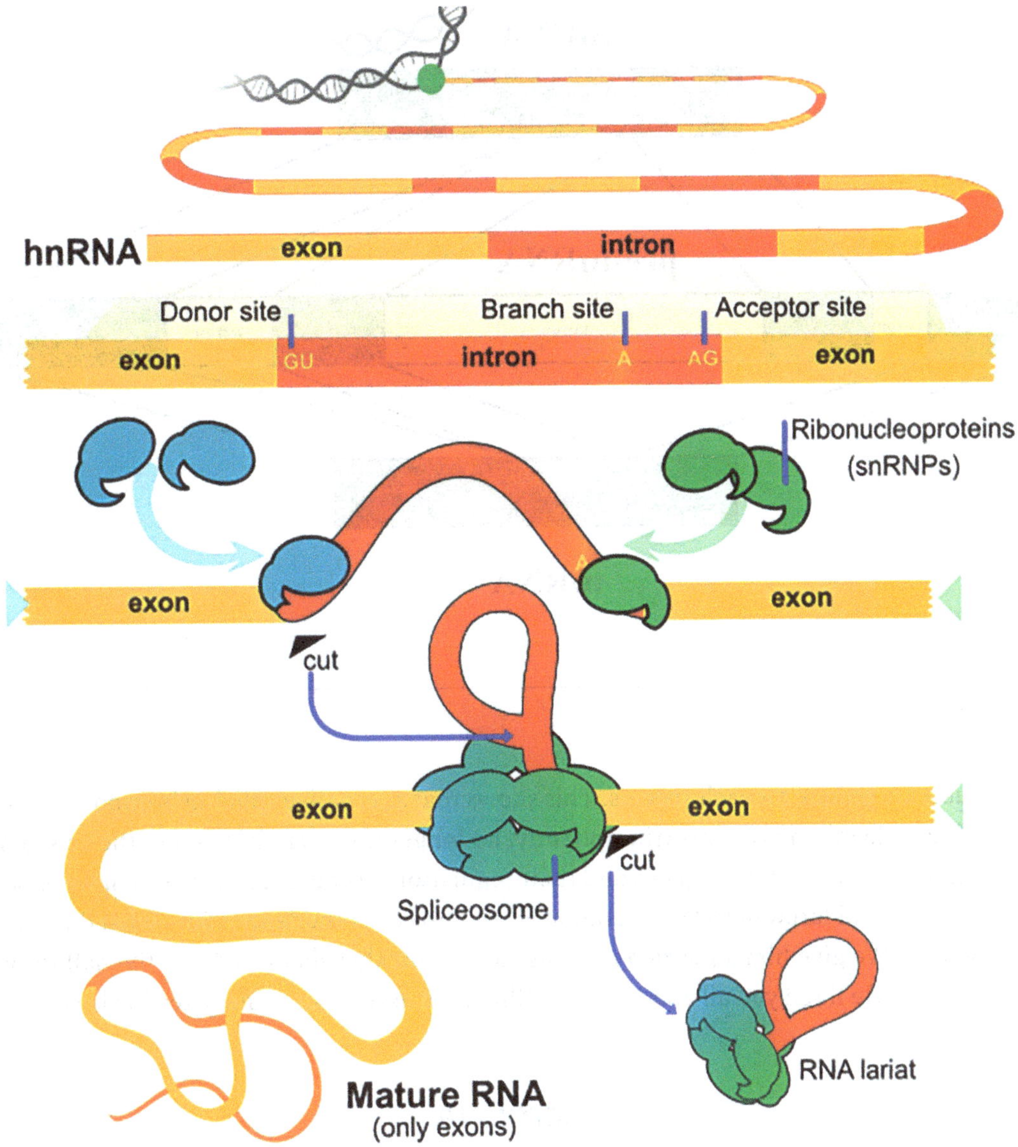

Figure 8.17

Spliceosome

Dr. Chambon explains that more than one messenger RNA can be produced by varying the number and combination of exons included in the spliced product. This is called **alternative splicing** and it greatly increases the diversity of proteins that can be encoded by the genome (see Figure 8.18). Amazingly, in humans, approximately 95% of split genes are alternatively spliced to produce multiple, related proteins. "It turns out that very similar genes are found in the same type of tissue—for example, the heart—in different species, as in humans and mice. BUT—the alternatively spliced

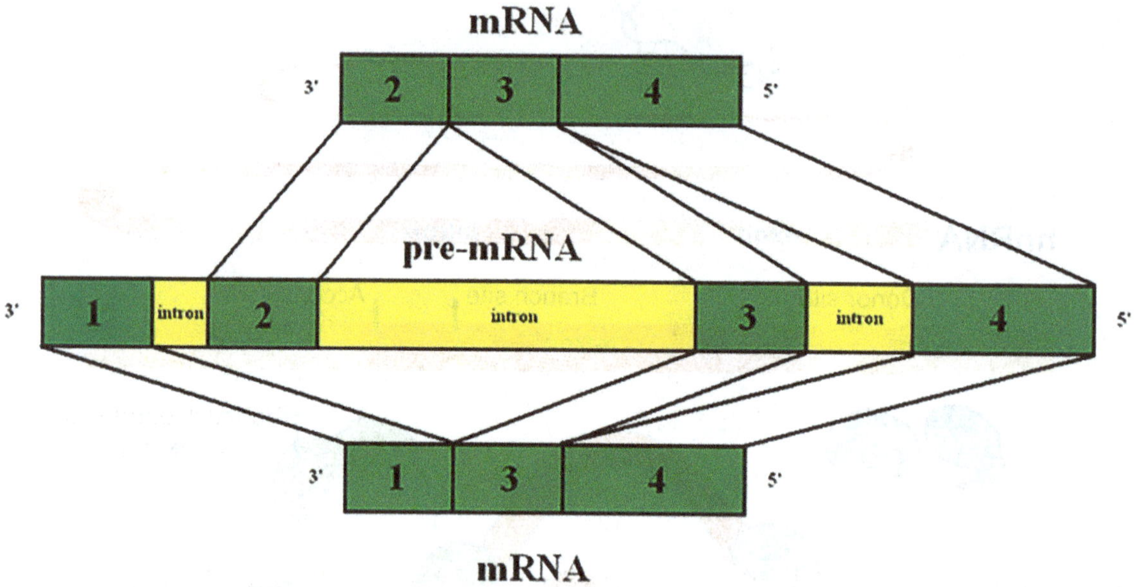

Figure 8.18

Alternative splicing

gene products are unique for each species. This shows that alternative splicing is important in gene evolution!" Dr. Chambon exclaims triumphantly, no longer (fortunately) waving the scissors. We are truly impressed. The study of genes and their regulation has taught us more than we expected.

We are about to bid farewell to Dr. Chambon when he asks us suddenly, "So—what do you think of micro RNA?" We give him a puzzled response as he quickly ushers us down the hall to see Dr. Victor Ambros. "He'll tell you all about it," Dr. Chambon assures us as he takes his leave.

microRNA

We arrive at Dr. Ambros's laboratory just in time to catch him peering anxiously at some small worms under the microscope. "We are looking for **microRNA**," we ask, assuming we're in the wrong place. Dr. Ambros assures us we have indeed found what we are looking for. "I have recently identified very small—22 bases long—regulatory RNAs that can bind to mRNAs in this worm and prevent them from being translated to protein," he explains. "At first, I thought it was a fluke ... err ... an anomaly, but then I found it in many forms of life, not just worms ... even humans! You have some, too!" he exclaims while peering at us very intently as if we were wearing them on our clothing. He then shows us the micro RNA from the worm *C. elegans* (see Figure 8.19).

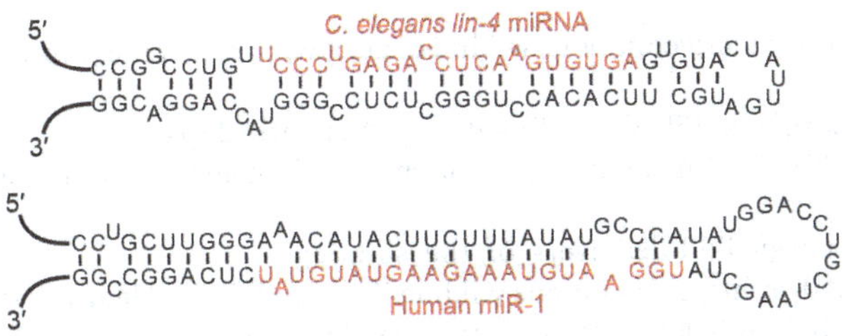

Figure 8.19.

microRNA

MicroRNAs (miRNAs) are transcribed from DNA and have been found to contain complementary regions that fold onto each other to produce a characteristic "hairpin" structure. MiRNAs act as gene silencers. They do so by complementary base pairing to the 3' end of the message that destabilizes the transcript. We now understand Dr. Ambros's excited state. A new level of regulation—genes that encode tiny RNAs that regulate the activity of mRNA—this is truly amazing!

It turns out that humans have about 1,000 different microRNAs that target more than 60% of genes. Dr. Ambros explains to us that certain types of human leukemia that involve the abnormal growth of white blood cells are caused by micro RNA dysregulation (see Figure 8.20). These abnormal micro RNAs are called **oncomirs** and are currently being studied in many types of cancer.

MicroRNA-21, or miR-21, is an oncomir that has been found at increased levels in many types of human cancer, including glioblastoma (brain cancer), breast, colorectal, lung, pancreas, skin, liver, gastric, cervical, thyroid, and lymphomas/leukemias. When present at abnormally high levels, this oncomir blocks the production of tumor suppressor proteins required for the regulation of cell growth. Now, suddenly, we are deeply impressed with the importance of gene regulation.

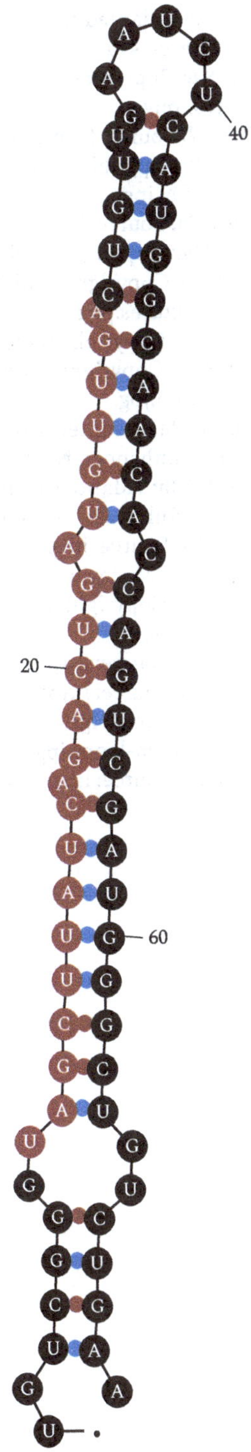

Figure 8.20

Human oncomir miR-21

Figure Credits

Fig. 8.1: Source: https://commons.wikimedia.org/wiki/File:Funny_Direction_Sign.Jpg

Fig. 8.3: Copyright © T A Raju (CC BY-SA 3.0) at https://commons.wikimedia.org/wiki/File:Lac_Operon.svg.

Fig. 8.4: Copyright © SocratesJedi (CC BY-SA 3.0) at https://commons.wikimedia.org/wiki/File:Annotated_Theoretical_Model_of_Bound_Tetrameric_Lac_Repressor.png.

Fig. 8.5: Adapted from Copyright © T A Raju (CC BY-SA 3.0) at https://commons.wikimedia.org/wiki/File:Lac_Operon.svg.

Fig. 8.6: Copyright © ArneLH (CC BY-SA 3.0) at https://commons.wikimedia.org/wiki/File:Gene_expression_control.png.

Fig. 8.7: Source: https://commons.wikimedia.org/wiki/File:Gene_Regulatory_Network_2.jpg

Fig. 8.8: Copyright © Sec11, trans. Eloquence (CC BY-SA 3.0) at https://commons.wikimedia.org/wiki/File:Plasmid_emEN.jpg.

Fig. 8.9a: Source: https://commons.wikimedia.org/wiki/File:Layers_of_the_skin.jpg

Fig. 8.9b: Copyright © Dhp1080 (CC BY-SA 3.0) at https://commons.wikimedia.org/wiki/File:Neuron.svg.

Fig.8.10: Copyright © Richard Wheeler (CC BY-SA 3.0) at https://commons.wikimedia.org/wiki/File:Chromatin_Structures.png.

Fig. 8.11: Copyright © OpenStax (CC BY 4.0) at https://commons.wikimedia.org/wiki/File:Figure_16_03_02.png.

Fig. 8.12: Copyright © Christoph Bock (CC BY-SA 3.0) at https://commons.wikimedia.org/wiki/File:DNA_methylation.jpg.

Fig. 8.13a: Adapted from Copyright © Jon Cheff (CC BY-SA 4.0) at https://commons.wikimedia.org/wiki/File:Enhancer_Nucleotide_Sequence.svg.

Fig. 8.13b: Adapted from Copyright © Jon Cheff (CC BY-SA 4.0) at https://commons.wikimedia.org/wiki/File:Enhancer_Nucleotide_Sequence.svg.

Fig. 8.14: Source: https://commons.wikimedia.org/wiki/File:De-Gene.png

Fig. 8.15: Source: https://commons.wikimedia.org/wiki/File:Pre-mRNA_to_mRNA.svg

Fig. 8.16: Copyright © BCSteve (CC BY-SA 3.0) at https://commons.wikimedia.org/wiki/File:RNA_splicing_reaction.svg.

Fig. 8.17: Source: https://commons.wikimedia.org/wiki/File:RNA_splicing_diagram_en.svg

Fig. 8.18: Source: https://commons.wikimedia.org/wiki/File:Alternativ_splicing.png

Fig. 8.19 : Copyright © VTD (CC BY-SA 4.0) at https://commons.wikimedia.org/wiki/File:Examples_of_microRNA_stem-loops.jpg.

Fig. 8.20: Source: https://commons.wikimedia.org/wiki/File:MiR-21_Structure.gif

Chapter 9

The Gene Pool

Figure 9.1

Penguin dives into pool

Natural Selection

It's a hot day in July, and we receive an invitation for a boat ride. Sounds like a great idea, so we hurry down to the dock. We are surprised to see a very large vessel with white sails billowing in the wind at port (see Figure 9.2).

Curious, we step aboard and find ourselves greeted by an elderly gentleman who—dressed in a long dark cape and top hat—in no way looks ready for a day at sea (see Figure 9.3). Nevertheless, we set sail and head for the Galápagos Islands off the coast of Ecuador.

Along the way Dr. Darwin (we surmise, as he failed to introduce himself) points out various mockingbirds, tortoises, and finches. "Remarkable," he repeats over and over again. They do, indeed, look very interesting, but "remarkable"? "How so?" we ask.

"Well, just look at those beaks," he says pointing to a group of finches. "Very nice," we agree, trying to sound enthusiastic. He shows us photographs of finches that live on several different Galápagos Islands (see Figure 9.4). "Each beak is different, because it is uniquely adapted to the feeding environments on the islands!"

Figure 9.2

The *HMS Beagle*

Figure 9.3

Charles Darwin

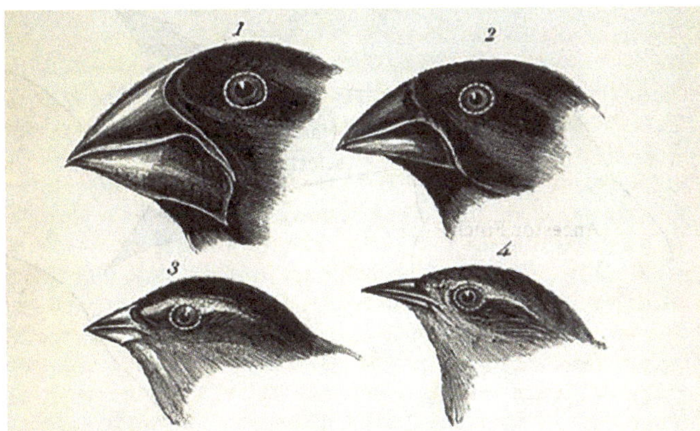

Figure 9.4

Darwin's finches from the Galápagos Islands

Figure 9.5

Natural selection in giraffes

"How do they exchange beaks?" we ask, slightly incredulous. Suddenly enraged, Dr. Darwin shouts, "Get off my ship!" We are shocked—surrounded by open seas, we see no exit—and wonder what has triggered this sudden outrage. "Don't you understand?" he explains, with a deliberate effort to calm himself down, **"This is survival of the fittest!"** We all settle down on deck as Dr. Darwin explains (see Figure 9.5).

So, now we begin to understand. The concept of **natural selection** means that environmental conditions that may vary geographically will favor the reproduction and survival of those individuals in a species that are most capable of thriving under these specialized circumstances. That's why it is called "survival of the fittest." If giraffes live in a forest with only very tall trees, only the tallest giraffes will be able to reach the leaves to obtain food. These tallest giraffes will be more likely to survive and reproduce. So—under these conditions—natural selection favors giraffes with very long necks. Over many generations, therefore, we will observe mostly giraffes with very long necks. This makes sense. "But what about Darwin's finches?" we ask. Darwin explains that the shape of the beak for finches living on different islands is different because of the need for these individual populations to adapt to different food sources (see Figure 9.6).

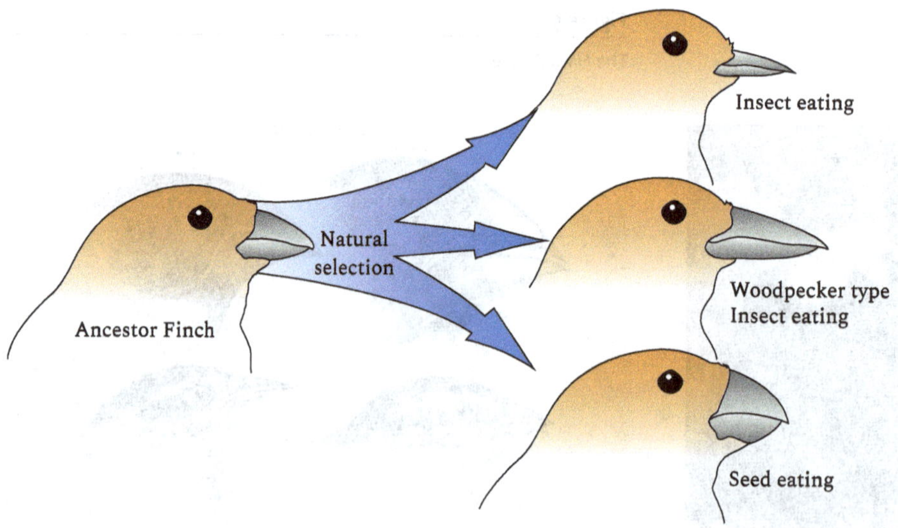

Figure 9.6

The effects of natural selection on beak shape in Darwin's finches

One general law, leading to the advancement of all organic beings, namely, multiply, vary, let the strongest live and the weakest die. (Darwin, 1859)

But why do these differences between individuals—that make them more or less fit for surviv-al—exist in the first place? Why aren't all members of a species the same? Dr. Darwin looks a bit perplexed, and then quickly ushers us off the ship. "You will have to talk to Dr. Hardy about that—I hear he's written a few interesting papers. He's over by the gene pool, relaxing." We thank Dr. Darwin and head for the pool, feeling pretty lucky that we may be able to take a quick dip on such a hot afternoon.

1. **Explain how the differing beak structures in the finches of the Galápagos Islands is an example of "natural selection."**
2. **What causes differences in beak shape in the finches?**

The Hardy Weinberg Equilibrium

Dr. G. H. Hardy is sitting by the pool sipping some lemonade and apparently involved in a deep conversation with another gentleman, whom we assume must be Dr. Wilhelm Weinberg. To our dismay, as we draw closer we overhear them arguing about who discovered the law. "What law?" we ask, suddenly interested in what's going on. "The Hardy Law!" one of the gentleman states emphatically. "No! It's the Weinberg Law!" shouts the other. Anxious to end this debate and cool off in the pool we suggest calling it "**The Hardy Weinberg Law**," which, fortunately, meets with their mutual approval. Now that this dispute is finally settled, we decide to ask the gentlemen more about this "law" that they obviously consider so important.

They explain that the Hardy Weinberg Law is all about the **gene pool**—meaning all the alleles that exist for every gene in a population. Although we humans—all members of the same species—have all the same genes, we don't all share the same alleles. Take a look at Figure 9.7. If we take all the genes and every allele associated with each gene for an entire population and put them in a huge imaginary container—that is the gene pool. The alleles in the gene pool contain all the possible genotypes and are a source of phenotypic variation in each new generation.

We now understand what the gene pool really is—it consists of all the alleles associated with every gene that are present in a population. All members of a species share the same genes, but the alleles associated with these genes may differ slightly in one individual from the next because of the occurrence of mutations that produce slight differences in phenotype. A population is a group of individuals—all from the same species—that pass their genes to the next generation by mating. In this way, the members of a population share the same gene pool. The alleles of all the individ-uals in a population determine both the allelic composition of the gene pool and the frequency of these alleles—the number of copies of one allele versus another associated with the same gene.

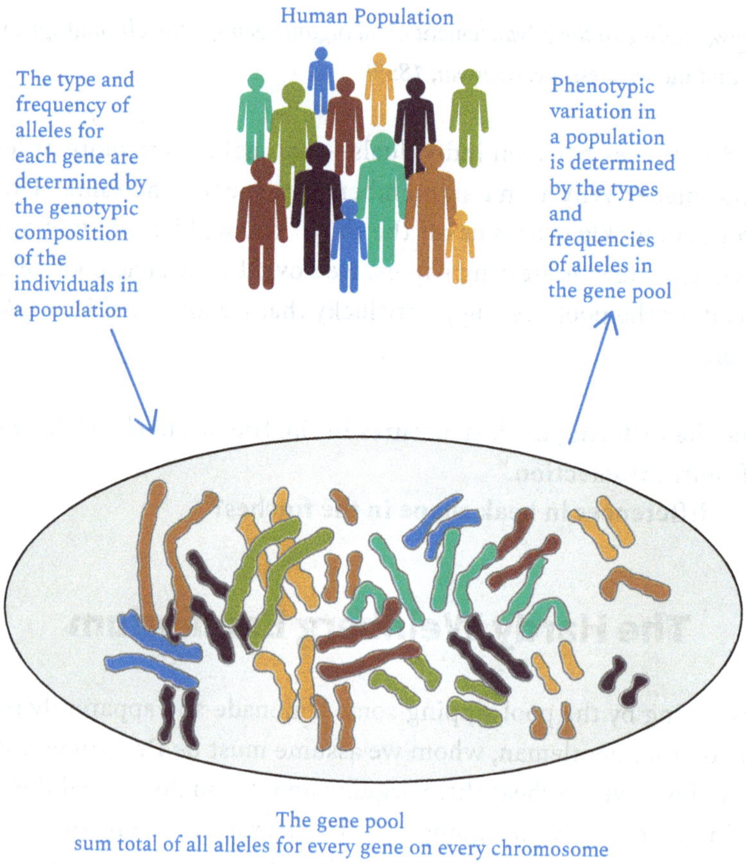

Figure 9.7

The gene pool

Factors Affecting Allelic Stability

Let's take a closer look at the relationship between genes and alleles (see Figure 9.8). Allelic variants of a gene originate as the result of mutations, changes in the base sequence of DNA that may affect the phenotype.

Mutations change the structure of a gene and are cause of allelic variation—the production of multiple alleles of a single gene. Most gene mutations are harmful because they produce errors in the genetic code. For example, single gene disorders may result from the loss of function of a mutant allele. Occasionally, however, mutations may produce alleles with positive phenotypic effects; for example, longer necks in giraffes make for better access to leaves in tall trees.

The concept that an allelic variant may have either a positive or negative effect on survival is called **fitness**. Fitness refers to the degree to which a phenotype associated with allelic variation affects reproductive survival; it is measured on a scale of 0 (lethal allele) to +1 (highest survival

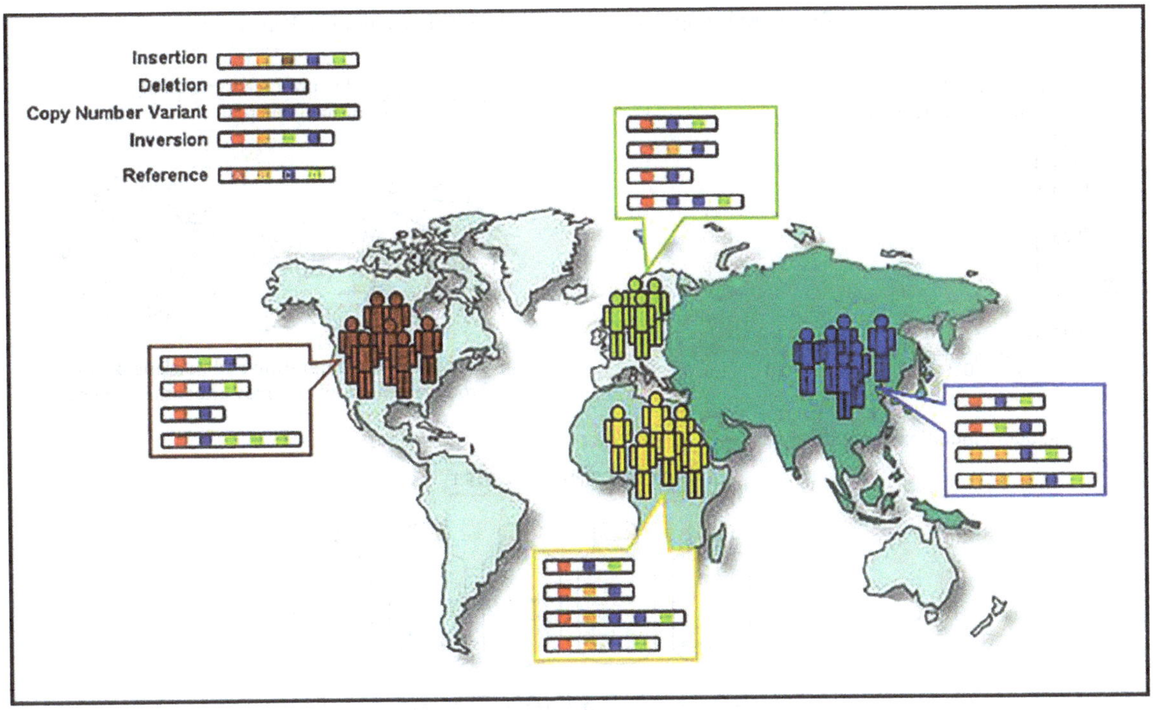

Figure 9.8

Allelic variation in human populations

advantage). The fact that allelic variants may alter the fitness of an individual means that their associated phenotypes may be subject to the forces of natural selection. The result may be a change in allelic frequency over time based on adaptation to the forces of natural selection.

So—what is required for allelic frequencies in a population to remain stable from one generation to the next (see Figure 9.9)?

3. **What are the characteristics of a population whose allelic frequencies are in equilibrium, and, therefore, do not change over time?**
4. **Explain how genetic drift and mutations contribute to changes in the gene pool over time.**

We wonder if allelic frequencies change over time in humans. What about the human gene pool? Does natural selection also occur in humans? We have been advised that Dr. Anthony Allison is heading to East Africa to study natural selection in humans and we decide to tag along. Dr. Allison is traveling on an extensive journey throughout sub-Saharan Africa to study the incidence of sickle cell disease (see Figure 9.10).

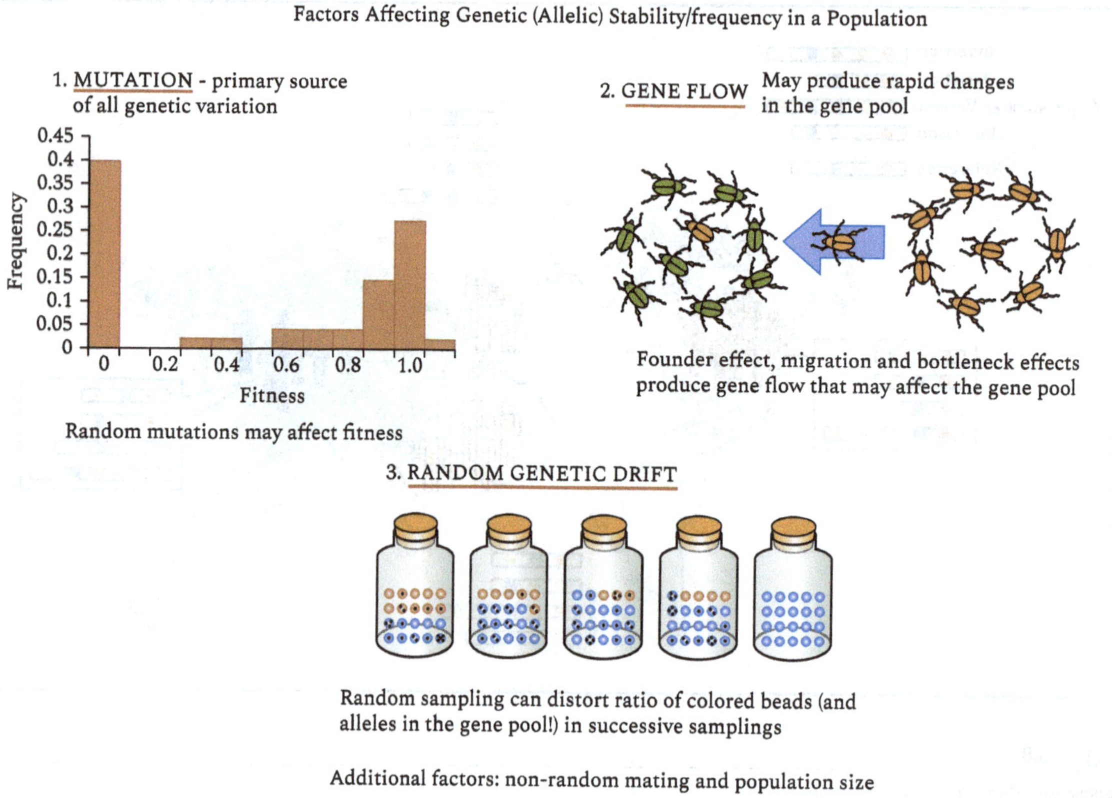

Figure 9.9

Factors affecting the frequency of alleles in the gene pool

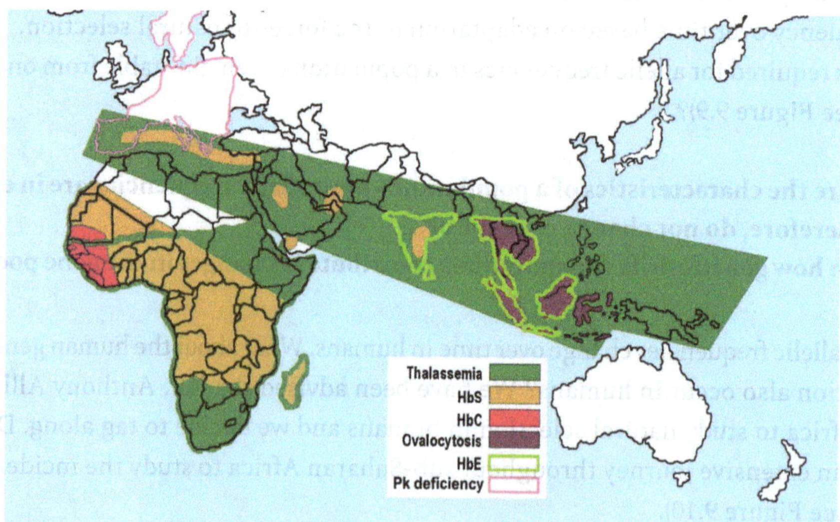

Figure 9.10

Distribution of sickle cell disease in Africa

We know that the disorder is caused by a point mutation that alters the structure of hemoglobin to produce sickle-shaped red blood cells that cause anemia, blood clots, and sometimes even death in untreated individuals. Dr. Allison is curious as to why the sickle cell allele is so common in this area of the world. "Its frequency is much higher than anywhere in Europe or the United States. I was wondering what could account for this difference." After extensive research, Dr. Allison finds that individuals who are carriers of the sickle cell allele are more resistant to the devastating consequences of malaria than individuals who have two copies of the normal allele. This is called **heterozygote advantage**, and accounts for the unusually high frequency of the sickle cell allele in areas of Africa where malaria is endemic. This is an adaptation to an environmental factor—malaria—that results in natural selection for carriers of the sickle cell allele.

We head back to the gene pool to discuss this exciting news with Dr. Hardy and Dr. Weinberg. We explain that Dr. Allison has informed us that the incidence of sickle cell disease in the Republic of the Congo is about 2%. "Can you tell us the frequency of the disease allele?" we ask. "Oh, yes, we can calculate the frequency of the sickle cell allele for you!" they state triumphantly. "It's very simple" (see Figure 9.11).

5. **In p + q = 1, what does p stand for?**
6. **In p = q = 1, what does q stand for?**
7. **In p2 + 2pq + q2 = 1, what does p2 stand for?**
8. **In p2 + 2pq + q2 = 1, what does 2pq stand for?**
9. **In p2 + 2pq + q2 = 1, what does q2 stand for?**

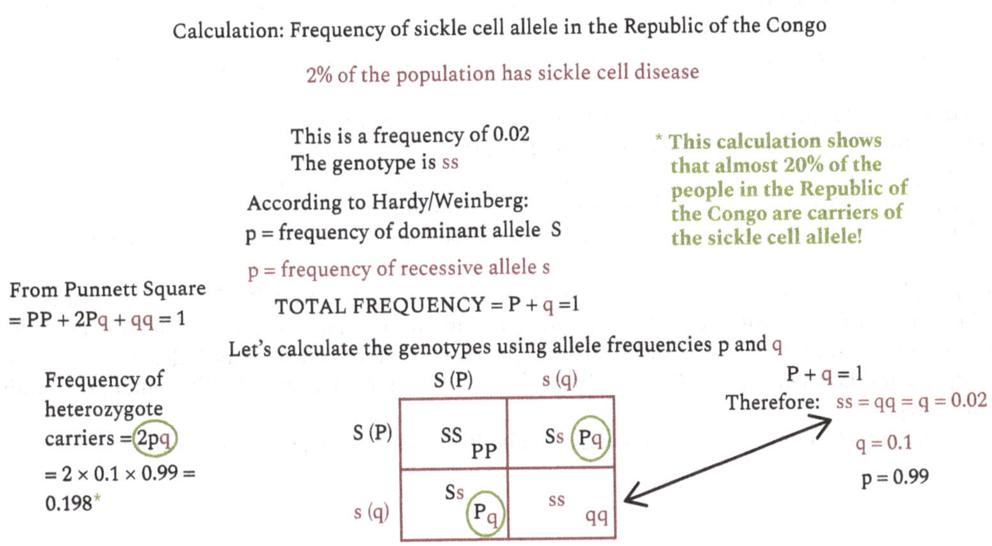

Figure 9.11

Tutorial: Calculation of allele frequencies

10. **If the number of individuals with the recessive disorder, cystic fibrosis, is 40 and the total population is 4 million: A. What is the frequency of the recessive CF allele in the population? B. What is the carrier frequency in this population?**

It has been an incredible journey! Dr. Allison's research has shown that the frequency of the sickle cell allele is directly affected by the incidence of malaria. This is a very dramatic example of how natural selection works in humans! We now understand how mutations cause changes in DNA sequence that produce multiple alleles of a single gene. Certain alleles may allow a survival advantage—survival of the fittest—depending on environmental conditions—natural selection—that will cause their frequency in the gene pool to increase over time. We leave Dr. Hardy and Dr. Weinberg at the gene pool where they appear to be arguing again—this time over which of them is the fittest.

> *We seem to be brought somewhat near to that great fact—that mystery of mysteries—the first appearance of new beings on this Earth. (Darwin, 1906)*

References

Darwin, Charles, *The Voyage of the Beagle*. No. 104. London: J. M. Dent & Sons, 1906.
Darwin, Charles, *On the Origin of the Species by Natural Selection*. London: 1859.

Figure Credits

Chapter 10

Who am I? ... The Human Genome

Figure 10.1

The human genome book

DNA Sequence Analysis

It's been an exciting adventure so far. Now it seems that things are getting even better! We have been invited to a lab where we will learn all about who we are—what's in our DNA and what it all means.

We hurry to the lab of Dr. Frederick Sanger, who invites us in with a warm welcome. Inside, we hear the whirring of large machines that are interspersed among many computers that seem to be everywhere. In fact, there's no one in sight—no sound except the quiet whirring noise of machines. "Where is everybody?" we ask. Dr. Sanger explains that we are the only ones here. "How do you get anything done in the lab?" we ask, surprised by the silence and the empty corridors. "People are not necessary—machines are doing all the work," is the reply. So—the machines are churning out the sequence of the genome—all the DNA that is found in every cell of a species (see Figures 10.1 and 10.2).

Today, researchers are sequencing the human genome. The results are almost ready. Dr. Sanger invites us to come inside and take a peek at the computer printout. Here is what it shows (see Figure 10.3).

We see a ribbon of brightly colored peaks and valleys streaming off the computer. When we inspect it more closely. We see that above each peak is a letter, either A, C, G, or T." Those are the DNA bases!" we exclaim. "We thought we were going to see the human genome." Dr. Sanger glances at us sideways before proceeding. "Yes, of course, those are the bases," he states blandly. Then, suddenly turning red, he

Figure 10.2

DNA sequencing machines

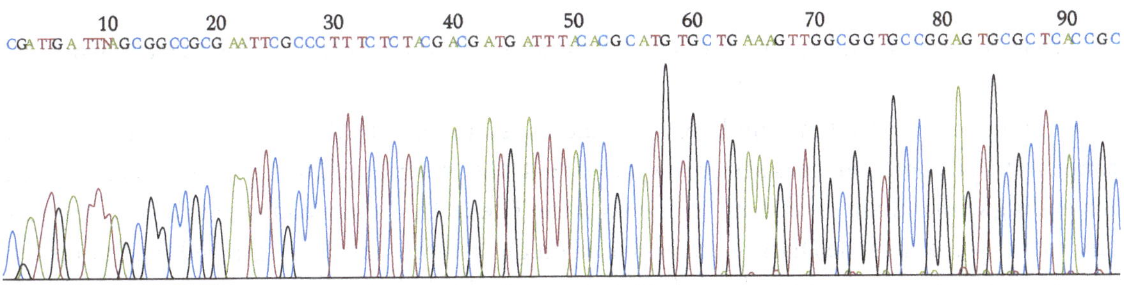

Figure 10.3

DNA chromatogram

jumps out of his chair and proclaims, "Do you realize what you are looking at??? This is the CODE OF LIFE!!!" We look at the printout again, as its significance begins to dawn on us. A simple readout of four bases—in any apparent order—is the blueprint for life on this planet. All life—humans and every other species on earth—shares this code. That such simplicity can create such complexity and diversity is unfathomable! We want to learn more about this. Fortunately, Dr. Sanger has regained his composure and seems willing to provide us with more details about this mysterious code.

1. **Why is the SEQUENCE or order of bases so important?**

DNA is extracted from the cell—any cell, because all cells in the body contain the same DNA—and broken into pieces. The sequence of bases comprising each piece is determined, and then all the pieces are put back together to determine the order of bases (3 billion!) for all 23 pairs of chromosomes in the human genome. "How does the computer distinguish one base from another to determine the sequence?" we ask. Dr. Sanger explains that he has just invented a method—which he modestly calls the Sanger Method—that uses base analogues called **dideoxy bases** to decipher the order of bases from 5' to 3' in any piece of DNA.

2. **How do dideoxybases allow us to determine the order of bases in DNA?**

He explains that the dideoxy bases are slightly modified from the original—they contain a hydrogen in place of the hydroxyl group at the 3' position of the deoxyribose sugar. Because DNA polymerase adds incoming bases to the 3'OH during replication, the dideoxy base serves as a chain terminator. The addition of bases cannot proceed further beyond the dideoxy base. Because each dideoxy base contains a different fluorescent label, the emission spectrum from that precise location along a DNA strand tells you which of the four bases is located at that position. "Isn't that amazing!" Dr. Sanger exclaims. "I can't believe I invented it!" We are duly impressed. Dr. Sanger then describes the process by which DNA sequencing is carried out in greater detail (see Figure 10.4).

3. **How do we determine which of the four dideoxy bases is at the end of a DNA strand?**

A test tube containing DNA template, the usual bases along with their dideoxy counterparts, a primer and DNA polymerase is set up to synthesize DNA. A series of DNA segments is produced, each ending with a chain-terminating dideoxy base. The DNA is then loaded onto a very thin capillary gel that separates the DNA segments based on their differences in length and the fluorescent labels occupying each position along the newly synthesized chain is scanned by laser detection and converted to a computer printout of the base sequence.

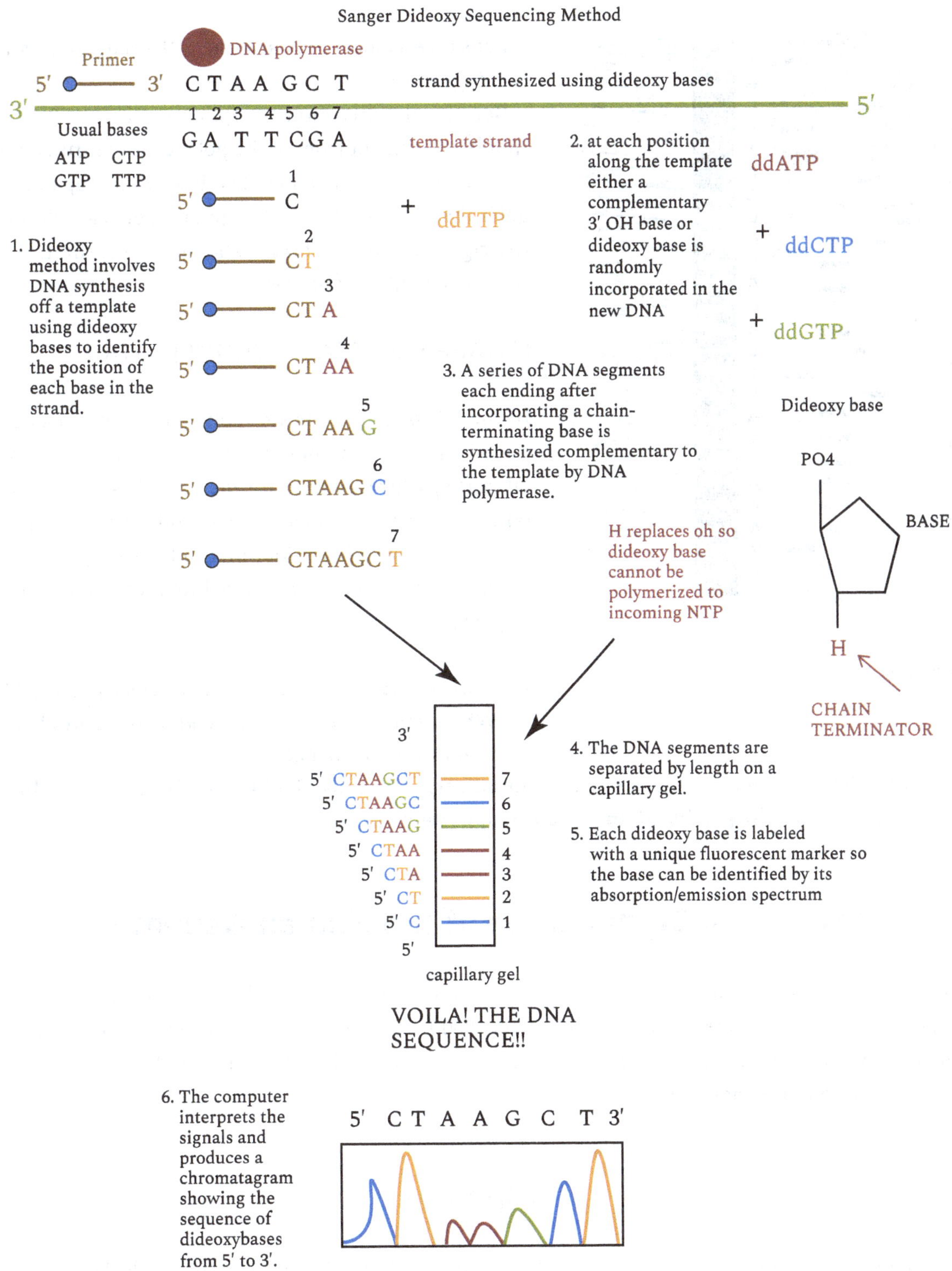

Figure 10.4

Tutorial: Dideoxy base sequencing method

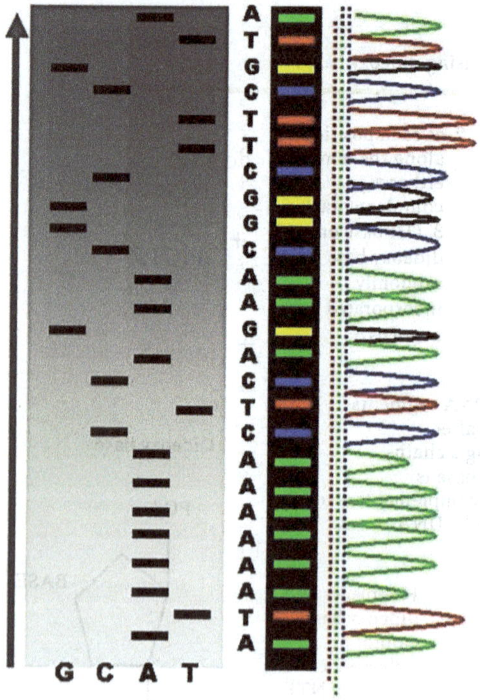

Figure 10.5

DNA sequence data

Let's take a closer look at some DNA sequence data (see Figure 10.5).

Because the direction of replication is 5' to 3', the first base at the bottom of the gel (because it runs the fastest) is the 5' end and the last base at the top of the gel is the 3' end of the DNA segment. For example, on the right side in the figure shown above, the DNA sequence reads as follows:

5'ATAAAAAACTCAGAACGGCTTCGTA 3'

In the left panel, the DNA sequence shown was deduced using radiolabeled 32P dideoxynucleotides. DNA is synthesized in four separate tubes, each containing a different dideoxy base, and then run separately on the gel. This older method has largely been replaced by the fluorescent labeling method of DNA sequencing.

4. **Why is it necessary to separate the DNA on a gel?**
5. **Why is the DNA sequence read 5' to 3' from bottom to top of the gel?**
6. **In a DNA sequence reaction, the template strand reads: 5'ATCGATCGATCG3' What sequence will be produced on the electropherogram?**

Structural Organization of the Human Genome

The Human Genome Project, a worldwide consortium that first determined the entire sequence of the human genome, was completed in the mid-2000s. The work continues today, as individual human genomes are sequenced and small differences associated with normal allelic variations as well as mutations are analyzed.

Transposons

We want to learn more about the structure of the human genome and are directed to the laboratory of Dr. Barbara McClintock for a further explanation (see Figure 10.6). When we finally locate her at Cold Spring Harbor Laboratory, she is outside working in the garden. As we walk over to introduce ourselves, we can't help but notice that she appears quite agitated. "I just can't find them! Oh—where did you go?" she keeps repeating, over and over again. Concerned that she may have lost something important, we inquire about the source of her agitation. "Did you lose something?" we ask politely. "Yes! My genes! I can't find my jumping genes—they keep getting away!" she exclaims. "What are jumping genes?" we ask, incredulous. Puzzled, we follow her back into the lab. "I'll show you what they look like, so you will recognize them if you see them," she explains.

Figure 10.6

Dr. Barbara McClintock in the genetics laboratory, Cold Spring Harbor, 1947.

Dr. McClintock explains that the structure of the human genome has been shaped by jumping genes—also called **transposons.** They can move around and determine the structure of the genome. She discovered them in maize—in her garden—and now has found that they were very important in shaping the human genome. Dr. McClintock explains how all this works (see Figure 10.7).

Jumping genes are actually a type of **insertion element (IS)**. Insertion elements can do just that—insert themselves into the DNA genome by means of an enzyme called a transposase encoded

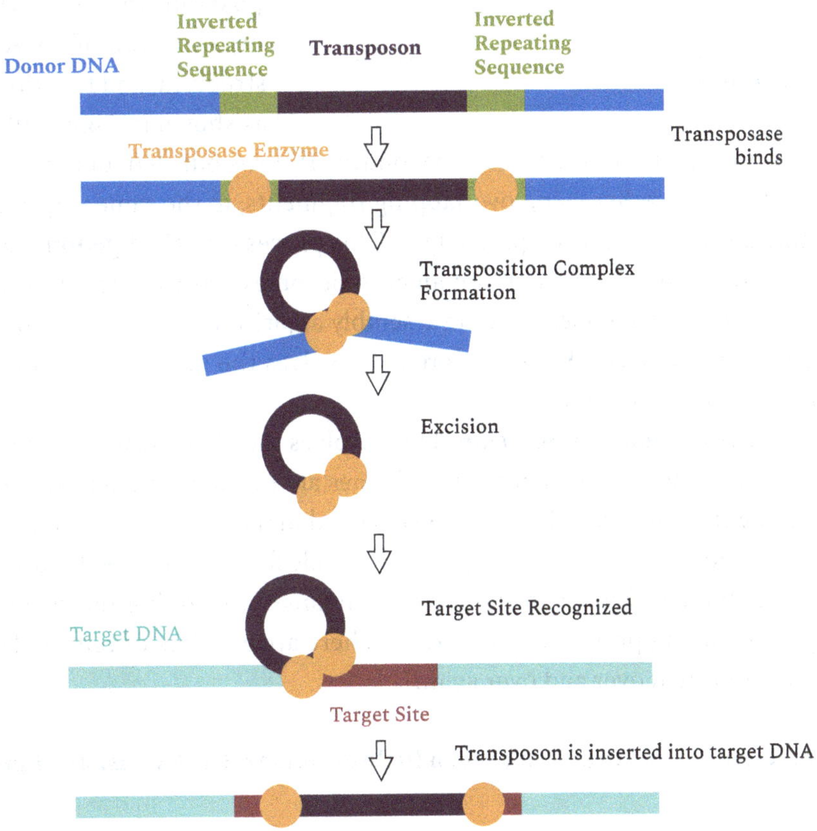

Figure 10.7

Jumping genes

by the element, and the DNA insertion segments located at either end of the IS. Many IS elements contain genes that they can insert anywhere in the genome. In this way, they can fashion the structural organization of the genome. IS elements comprise over 25% of the human genome.

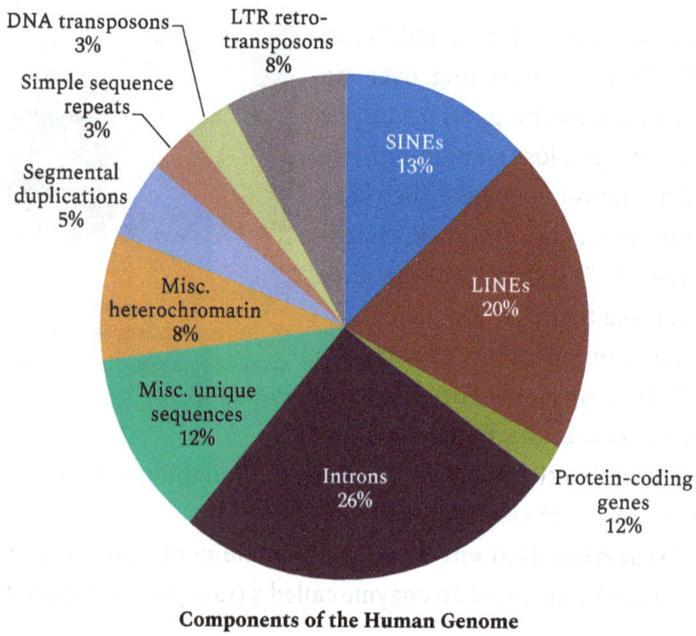

Figure 10.8

Annotation of the human genome

Studying the Human Genome

When the human genome sequencing project was complete, it was possible to assign the structural organization of DNA to numerous structural and functional categories, as shown in Figure 10.8.

How was all this information assembled, we wonder? It turns out that all the sequenced DNA segments were put back together using overlapping fragments, in the same way you put a puzzle together from tiny pieces with overlapping edges. This process is called **genome assembly**. The DNA sequence of each of the 23 pairs of human chromosomes was assembled to show the exact sequence of DNA bases on each one. Genome assembly algorithms assist in this process done by computer. This is called **structural annotation** and involves the identification of the structural elements in DNA and their locations.

The next step is called **genome annotation.** This involves the identification of which DNA segments encode protein, which are regulatory, which ones are repeat elements, etc. This represents a structural assessment of biological information encoded in the DNA. Only a small percentage of the human genome—about 1.5%—contains genes that code for proteins (see Figure 10.8). A much larger percentage of human DNA is in the form of introns—noncoding intervening sequences that are interspersed among protein coding exons. There are also lots of repeat elements—base sequence segments repeated over and over again.

7. **Why were scientists so surprised that so little of human DNA consists of protein coding genes?**
8. **Why are introns important?**

We humans have about 20,000 protein coding genes and lots of segments that are repeated many times. In fact, segment duplications occur frequently and can be used to map the relationship between different groups of people based on the similarities and differences in segment duplication patterns. The **HapMap Project** was set up by the National Institutes of Health (NIH) to catalog the common variants in European, East Asian, and African genomes.

Figure 10.9 shows the worldwide distribution of the blood type A allele. The multiple alleles for blood type appear to have evolved from a single primordial gene and show a distinctive frequency pattern among the major geographical areas of the world.

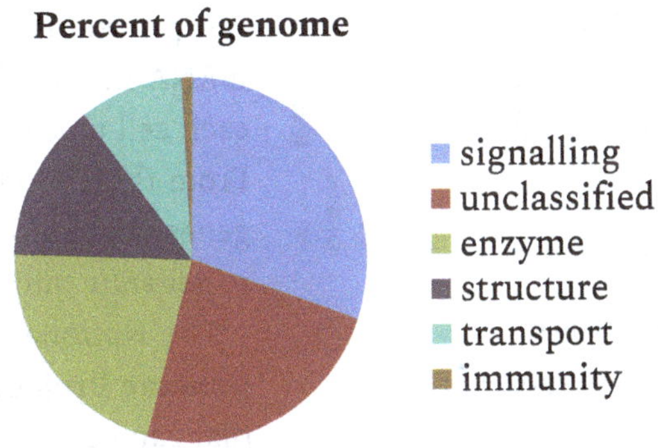

Figure 10.9

Worldwide distribution of the blood type A allele

Functional Analysis of the Human Genome

Functional annotation of the human genome involves an assessment of the biological functions of genes and how they are regulated (see Figure 10.10).

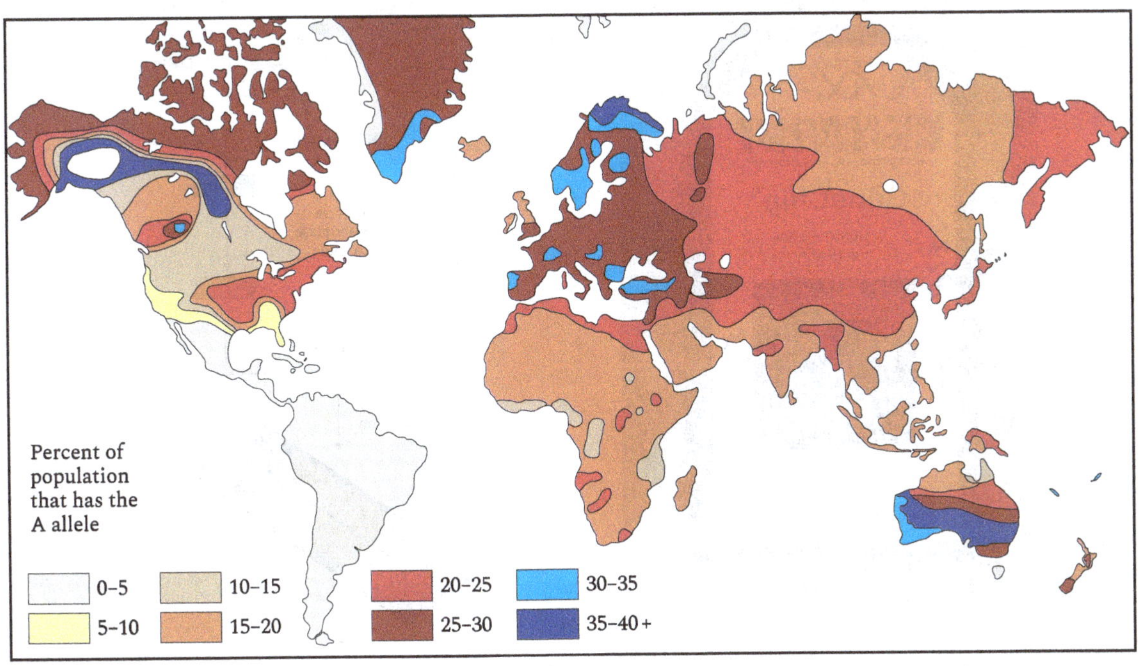

Figure 10.10

Functional annotation of the human genome

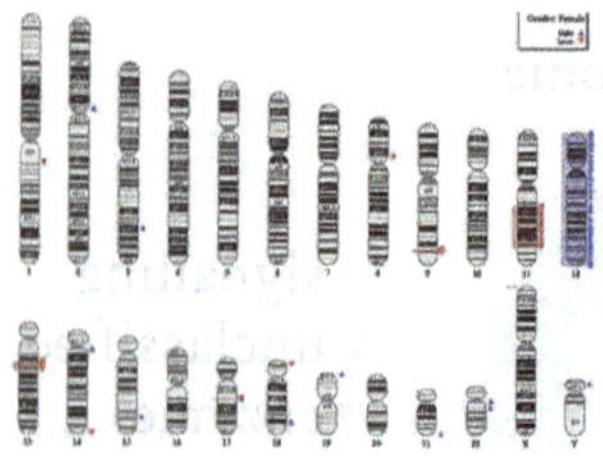

Figure 10.11

Virtual karyotype

A procedure called **RNA-seq** allows researchers to sequence the mRNA in cells. This allows us to see the mRNA composition within each cell type as it contributes to tissue diversity and specialization. From these studies, we have learned that more than 90% of human genes can be alternatively spliced into different combinations of exons to generate multiple mRNAs from a single gene.

The National Institutes of Health (NIH) established the **Cancer Genome Project** that is involved in identifying all the human genes that can be associated with different types of cancer. Patient tumors are analyzed for gene mutations that may have contributed to tumor development. Figure 10.11 shows a virtual karyotype from a young patient with leukemia. A virtual karyotype is prepared using small segments of DNA that are sequenced and then assigned to their correct location on a standard karyotype. This provide a fine map of gene structure. This virtual karyotype shows all the chromosomal locations where mutations were pinpointed in this patient.

How do we determine the functional differences between a normal genome and one that contains mutant cancer causing genes? A technology involving the use of "gene chips" has helped to answer this question (see Figure 10.12).

Let's see how this procedure works. Figure 10.13 shows that total messenger RNA is first extracted from normal cells and tumor cells of the same tissue type. A DNA copy of each mRNA

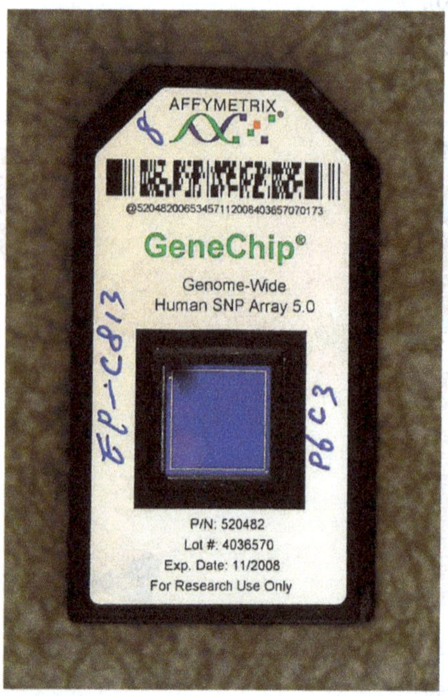

Figure 10.12

Gene chip

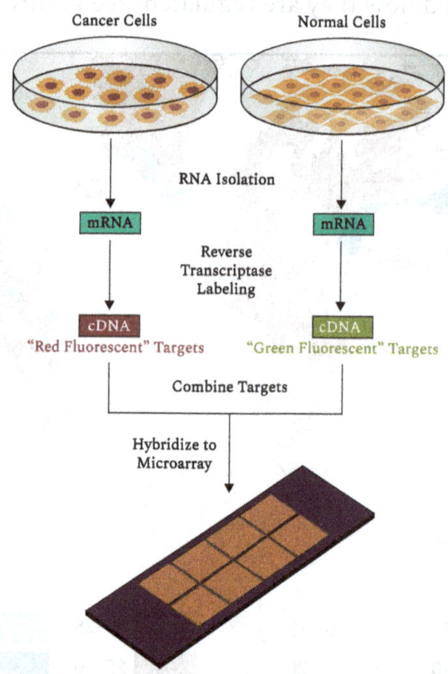

Figure 10.13

Microarray preparation

[called complementary DNA or cDNA] is made using an enzyme called reverse transcriptase that makes DNA from RNA. The cDNA from tumor cells and normal cells is then labeled with different fluorescent tags [red or green] to distinguish them. They are then hybridized to a gene chip that contains all the protein coding genes in the human genome. Hybridization involves complementary base pairing between the single-stranded cDNA and the genes in single-stranded form on the gene chip. The product is called a **microarray**. The pattern and intensity of the fluorescent spectrum indicates which genes are expressed in the normal versus the tumor cells.

The microarray data shown in the Figure 10.14 shows the pattern of gene expression in leukemia cells from patients with pediatric B-cell lymphoblastic leukemia tested before and after chemotherapy treatment. The microarray analysis reveals a change in gene expression of mRNA in tumor cells before and after treatment in several children with leukemia. Red fluorescence indicates high-level messenger RNA expression; green fluorescence indicates low-level expression of mRNAs encoded by specific genes. These microarray data show that the pattern of gene expression in the cancer cells is altered following treatment with chemotherapy. Moreover, the pattern of gene expression posttreatment shown on the right panel is comparable with a normal lymphoid cell. These data can be used to assess the therapeutic effects of drug treatment at the genetic level. In this case, the microarray assessment shows that the treatment has disrupted the abnormal growth pattern of the tumor cells by restoring a normal pattern of gene expression. Taken together,

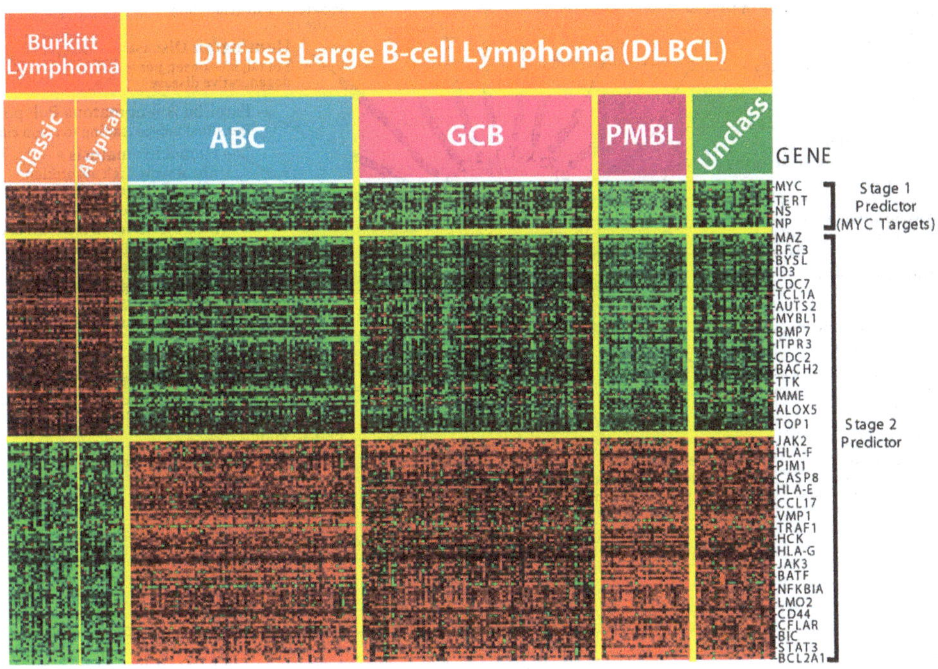

Figure 10.14

Microarray data

the microarray data produced by gene chip hybridization is called the **gene expression signature**, because the analysis provides the combined gene expression profile for the cell.

9. Does a gene chip contain all the DNA from a genome?

Gene chip microarray analysis is an extremely useful tool for studying complex disorders—such as cancer—in which many genes may be implicated in producing the abnormal phenotype. For the many genetic disorders involving defects limited to a single gene, the Human Genome Project has revealed their chromosome locations and has also identified the base sequence mutations associated with these single gene disorders (see Figure 10.15). Research databases have shown that, of approximately 25,000 annotated genes in the human genome, mutations in more than 3,000 genes have been associated with genetic disorders.

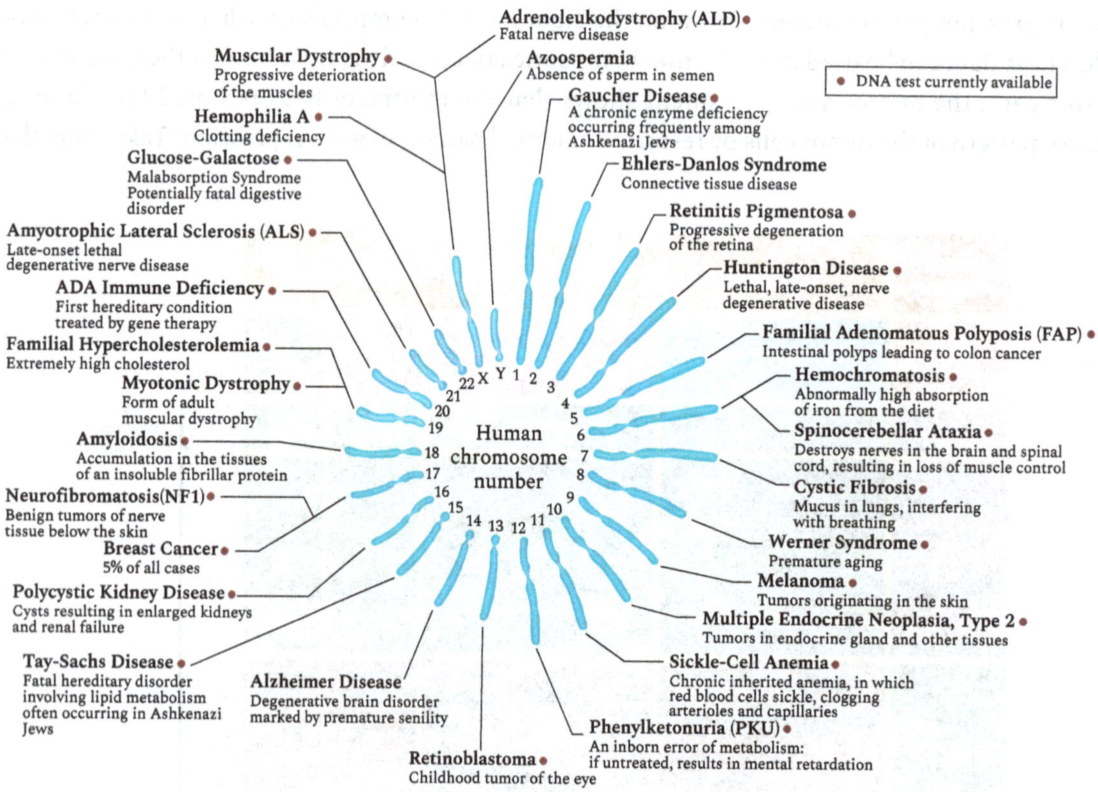

Figure 10.15

Human disease genes

Looking Toward the Future

Our journey is almost over. It has been an adventure in space and time as we have explored the world of genetics. Our last appointment is with the future, as we take a leap forward to see what lies ahead. Today we visit the laboratory of Dr. Jennifer Doudna and Dr. Emmanuelle Charpentier, inventors of a new technology, "clustered regularly interspaced short palindromic repeats," or Crispr-cas9 (see Figure 10.16). Crispr are short repeated DNA palindromes (DNA sequences that read the same in both 5' and 3' directions) that were originally discovered in bacteria. Dr. Charpentier explains that Crispr sequences are part of the bacterial immune system. DNA from virus invaders is found in between the Crispr repeats. If the same virus invader attempts to attack the bacterial cells again, the inserted viral DNA can target the invading virus via base-pair recognition. Using a protein called cas9, the bacteria literally slice up the invading virus by making double stranded cuts in its DNA. "That is truly remarkable!" we exclaim. "It's like genetics star wars."

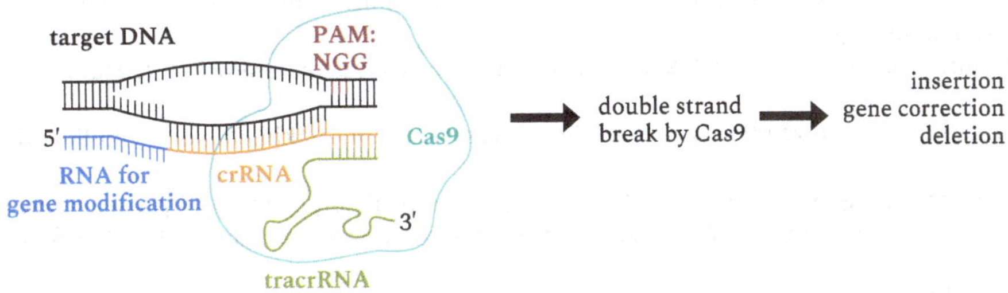

Figure 10.16

Crispr-Cas9 gene editing

"We realized that this bacterial immune response could be adapted to edit genes in any type of cell—even human cells," Dr. Doudin explains. The researchers designed specific short RNAs that can base pair to any DNA segment that needs to be edited by simple base-pair recognition. The attached Cas9 molecular scissors cut the DNA at the targeted site and host repair enzymes either add a new DNA segment or remove it, depending on the type of mutation that needs correcting. "Does this mean you can correct mutations that cause genetic diseases?" we ask excitedly. "Not yet," Dr. Charpentier cautions. She explains that there is more work that needs to be done to ensure that only the targeted gene is altered and that the corrective repair mechanism is

Figure 10.17

Evening walk

highly accurate. "We are only at the beginning of a very long journey," she adds ruefully. "But we will get there!"

Yes, we will. We are very anxious to continue our exploration, but the sun is setting, the light grows dim, and we realize we must wait for another day to begin again.

Figure Credits

Fig. 10.1: Copyright © Stephencdickson (CC BY-SA 4.0) at https://commons.wikimedia.org/wiki/File:The_Genome_sequence_when_printed_fills_a_huge_book_of_close_print.JPG.

Fig. 10.2: Copyright © Scotted400 (CC BY-SA 3.0) at https://commons.wikimedia.org/wiki/File:Illumina_Hiseq_2000_sequencers,_BGI_Hong_Kong_sequencing_room.JPG.

Fig. 10.3: Source: https://commons.wikimedia.org/wiki/File:Sanger_sequencing_read_display.png

Fig. 10.5: Copyright © Abizar (CC BY-SA 3.0) at https://commons.wikimedia.org/wiki/File:Radioactive_Fluorescent_Seq.jpg.

Fig. 10.6: Source: https://commons.wikimedia.org/wiki/File:Barbara_McClintock_(1902-1992)_shown_in_her_laboratory_in_1947_-_Original.jpg

Fig. 10.7: Copyright © Alana Gyemi (CC BY-SA 4.0) at https://commons.wikimedia.org/w/index.php?curid=54955687.

Fig. 10.8: Copyright © Alglascock (CC BY-SA 3.0) at https://commons.wikimedia.org/wiki/File:Components_of_the_Human_Genome.jpg.

Fig. 10.9: Copyright © Boghog (CC BY-SA 4.0) at https://commons.wikimedia.org/wiki/File:Human_genome_function.svg.

Fig. 10.10: Copyright © Muntuwandi (CC BY-SA 3.0) at https://commons.wikimedia.org/wiki/File:Map_of_blood_group_a.gif.

Fig. 10.11: Copyright © Jhagenk (CC BY-SA 3.0) at https://en.wikipedia.org/w/index.php?curid=21902577.

Fig. 10.12: Copyright © Ricardipus (CC BY-SA 2.0) at https://commons.wikimedia.org/wiki/File:Affymetrix_5.0_microarray.jpg.

Fig. 10.13: Source: https://commons.wikimedia.org/wiki/File:Microarray-schema.gif

Fig. 10.14: Source: https://commons.wikimedia.org/wiki/File:DNA-microarray_analysis.jpg

Fig. 10.15: Source: https://commons.wikimedia.org/wiki/File:Human_chromosome_diseases_set_en.png

Fig. 10.16: Copyright © ViktoriaAnselm (CC BY-SA 4.0) at https://commons.wikimedia.org/wiki/File:CRISPR-Cas9_mode_of_action.png.

Fig. 10.17: Thomas Creswick, "The Evening Walk," http://www.racollection.org.uk/ixbin/indexplus?record=O13503&session=Q6xsxbvDg0P. 1842.